THE BEST OF BOTH WORLDS
MILLIONAIRE
Mum

Diane McKendrick

First published by Ultimate World Publishing 2021
Copyright © 2021 Diane McKendrick

ISBN

Paperback: 978-1-922597-65-6
Ebook: 978-1-922597-66-3

Diane McKendrick has asserted her rights under the Copyright, Designs and Patents Act 1988 to be identified as the author of this work. The information in this book is based on the author's experiences and opinions. The publisher specifically disclaims responsibility for any adverse consequences which may result from use of the information contained herein. Permission to use information has been sought by the author. Any breaches will be rectified in further editions of the book.

All rights reserved. No part of this publication may be reproduced, stored in or introduced into a retrieval system, or transmitted in any form, or by any means (electronic, mechanical, photocopying, recording or otherwise) without the prior written permission of the author. Any person who does any unauthorised act in relation to this publication may be liable to criminal prosecution and civil claims for damages. Enquiries should be made through the publisher.

Cover design: Ultimate World Publishing
Layout and typesetting: Ultimate World Publishing
Editor: Alex Floyd-Douglas

Ultimate World Publishing
Diamond Creek,
Victoria Australia 3089
www.writeabook.com.au

DEDICATION

To all the Mumma's out there, past, present and future who are doing their best: It's time to let go of all the things we have been taught and unleash our true selves to the world.

I lost myself to motherhood and became Ross and Esme's Mum and Gus' Wife, but I have more to me than that. I have a gift of reminding and reflecting to others their magic, creativity and connection. I also have a sixth sense in creating and cultivating a conscious community.

My dream is to facilitate and guide you to living YOUR dreams!

Whatever they may be.

Most of us have lost ourselves along the way somewhere; in our work, an illness, job, parenting, relationship, business, in an endless pursuit to prove ourselves. I know because I have done it and worked with hundreds of women who have also made what they do, who they are.

Our families can be a huge part of our purpose in life, but we need to know who WE are first, so we can show up as

OURSELVES in our parenting, business, and finances. And not be who we think we "should be" or who others expect us to be. If we do it the other way around, it's a long hard slog (I know that because I have done that, too!).

This book is a dedication to any woman out there who is feeling lost, lonely, or isolated (even if you're pretending you're not) on the hamster wheel and feeling fundamentally flawed like there is something wrong with you.

Alternatively, you feel peachy and ready to take next leap but feel fear and sabotage creeping in… Whatever your why, I'm here to help you all!

REMEMBER: YOU ARE AMAZING! Before the motherhood, before the money, before the mindset.

Just simply by being YOU! Your true magic resides within.

Everything on the outside is a reflection of your self-worth.

Close your eyes, take a deep breath, and put your hand on your heart.

Listen deeply and if you want more from life, boil the kettle, put your feet up and keep reading. You CAN have your cake and eat it, too.

Welcome to your life of freedom, abundance and living your deepest desires.

Love and light,
Diane

CONTENTS

Dedication	iii
Introduction	1
1. Your Time Is NOW	19
2. Finding The Genius Within	41
3. "X"Marks the Spot: Soul Purpose	61
4. Bridge The Gap To A Higher Standard: Values	79
5. Frozen: Conquering FEAR	97
6. Wrong Way: Go Back And Drop The B/S"	119
7. Magic Morning Routine: Super Charge Your Day	133
8. Manifesting Magician: Find Your Magic	155
9. Absolute Abundance	173
10. Compelling New Identity: You Are Her And She Is YOU	197
Acknowledgements	213
About The Author	217
Diane McKendrick – Speaker	221
Testimonials	223
Journey With Me And Join My Conscious Community	229

INTRODUCTION

Welcome to Millionaire Mum!

This is where you can create and design the life of your dreams. Where you can have your cake and eat it, too! You can even choose the flavour you love... Chocolate, cheesecake, gluten-free, dairy-free, vegan... Whatever your heart desires.

No one is here to judge you or tell you that "you can't do that," or think you're a weirdo because you don't like cake and would rather eat a banana - well maybe that is a bit weird to some of you, but even as a kid, I was never that keen on cake!

I remember sitting in my office job at Cannon Hill Kmart Plaza where I was the receptionist of the shopping centre. Our office was right next to The Cheesecake Shop so the smell of baking cakes filled the air every morning. At least once a week we would sit down to morning tea with the staff and while they all enjoyed their Lemon Meringue Pie, I would be just as satisfied eating my banana…

Okay, now it's time to cut the crap! Stop criticising and competing against yourself and each other. It's time to cheer loudly and wholeheartedly for the next woman, and of course, yourself.

My name is Diane McKendrick. I am a driven, focused, successful businesswoman who is also a soft, nurturing, wise, feminine goddess. I am a Boss-Babe-Thriving-Business-Owner and a wholesome-dance-in-the-kitchen and read-them-bedtime-stories-kinda-mum.

I go from business meetings to school drop off. I go from dining in some of the finest restaurants with extremely influential people to eating sandy fish and chips on the beach with my family and dreadlocks in my hair. I go from speaking, motivating and inspiring humans all over the world to pulling my hair out when my own children refuse to listen to a word I say. It drives me bonkers!

The contrast is stark.

I'm writing this book to show you that you can have it all.

You CAN do what you love with people you love and create an impact in the world, adding value to people's lives and receiving financial abundance. You CAN create, call in and

Introduction

make a shit ton of money AND you can do bed time stories, morning pancakes, school pick up and drop offs, book week, school lunches and dinners. You CAN take days off when your children are sick, spend your nights with family camp fires and slowly wake each morning spending sacred time with your special, little people.

Sounds good, right? This CAN be you.

All you have to do is choose it! Right now, in this moment, choose your path forward and boldly declare it to yourself and the universe. This is where your dream life begins.

It's time now to wake up. To stop subscribing to society and Western Culture, following the rules and living inside the box. To make a decision and choose the Millionaire Mum way of life.

Success means different things to different people. It is my intention through this book and our time together for you to feel crystal clear on what success and abundance means to YOU. Your version; not what society has taught you.

Should you decide to join this journey with me, be prepared for monumental growth. It is time to connect with your internal compass, to create and align with your vision of success and abundance in ALL areas of your life.

For many years, I thought success was the number on the scales or the amount in the bank account; the gold medal, the promotion at work, the job, the car, the house... I've come to understand now that was all on the 'outside of me.'

Having been a Gold Medal Athlete at National Level, I believed success required sacrifice and I could not have it all. If I had it all, I was greedy or selfish. This is where my limiting belief that I could either be a Millionaire OR a Mum was born. I would tell myself religiously that I could not possibly have both AND do both well.

I was driven, focused, disciplined and I was programmed to WIN. At all costs.

Often in my earlier years, winning cost me dearly. My health suffered as I pushed so hard. I got chronic fatigue, my friendships and relationships fell apart as I would only have time for work or training. I started to drink a lot of alcohol and fell into deep depression. I put on a brave face as I plummeted into a dangerous out-of-control spiral. I convinced myself that no one cared.

After years of chasing the dream life, I got a promotion to move to Sydney as Portfolio Manager of several shopping centres. I said "yes," thinking that the income and status was the WIN; the reward and success I had been craving. As I was walking past the Real Estate office under my office building, I caught a glimpse of my reflection in the glass window. I was dressed in a designer suit, with very expensive (and matching) shoes and handbag, juggling a briefcase, my Blackberry and balancing my takeaway coffee. This was my subconscious version of 'success' as I had seen in so many movies growing up.

Fortunately for me, that day was different. Something happened that snapped me out of my slumber.

Introduction

I heard a voice that said, *"Is this all there is?"*

In that moment, I realised I was living someone else's dream. Married to my job, creating an identity around what I did, not who I was. I was on autopilot, thinking I was happy but slowly dying on the inside.

From that day, I made some big changes. I quit my job, I started attending every personal development seminar I could find. I read books and listened to podcasts. I swapped alcohol for kombucha, wild dance parties for yoga sessions and toxic relationships for time with myself.

It was the best decision of my life.

Fast forward several years later and I met my now husband, Gus. It was the classic love at first sight - and not long after meeting, we got married and had children.

Even at this point in my life, I was still extremely focused and driven. I was very competitive and maintained my win-at-all-costs attitude. Possibly a little stubborn, verging on pig-headed and extremely impatient with impossible expectations of myself and anyone else in my vortex.

I realised quickly after having my two children, Ross and Esme, motherhood called for something softer, something slower, something more aligned. To be honest, I struggled big time with this. My little humans have taught me so much.

Presence, patience, persistence, peace, and most of all, true love.

Millionaire Mum

With Gus working away in his dream job as an International Airline Pilot for Virgin, I would often have sleepless nights with the kids. I loved raising my children and it was a dream come true. So, it was surprising to me when I got really honest with myself.

I felt lonely, isolated and stagnant.

I had a fantasy of what being 'Mum' would be like and much like my past, I was searching for fulfillment outside of me; this time in my motherhood.

Why was I feeling so helpless?

I had my dream life. An amazing husband, and healthy, happy, albeit challenging and spirited children. But those 3am wake ups to breastfeed when the world was still and quiet, I had an empty feeling in the pit of my stomach.

The days were busy, too busy to feel the emptiness. I busied myself with being the best Mum I knew how. I still felt the dread of not being enough. The reality of being at home with small children hit hard. Dirty nappies, sleepless nights, with my body changing. Every model of the world I had created came crashing down around me. I became Ross and Esme's mum and Gus' wife.

I had still not discovered the Golden Goose of Inner Peace, deep within ME.

I would dream about what else I could do with my life. As I was dreaming, I noticed I started to feel guilty. I wanted

Introduction

an identity outside of motherhood, I wanted to contribute financially to our family, and I wanted to help others. As much as I loved my children, I started to notice I also wanted a purpose outside of being a mum. I wanted to leave a legacy outside the family unit, as well as within it.

I wanted to get to know ME.

With the support of Gus and my Mum, I started a Personal Training Business training other Mum's, which took off. Often with Esme attached to my front and Ross in a hiking pack on my back, I would train Mum's all day long. Overall, I started to feel a bit better, however the long nights of breast feeding and then working all day started to take its toll on my mental health.

Today, I see my business as my third child. As we grow as a family, the business grows with us. I have transitioned my business from Personal Training where we just work on the body to a more wholesome approach to life. I am now a Life Coach, Motivational Speaker and Best-Selling Author of my first book, *Rise Up, The Soulful Guide to Success*.

I work predominantly with other mothers and my business has boomed. As it kept scaling beyond my wildest dreams, I noticed something coming up for me. A deep-seeded limiting belief that to have a successful million-dollar business AND be a total Boss-Babe Mum meant that the growth of my business would at the expense of my mothering and parenthood. I felt it meant that I couldn't possibly be, do and have it all. A million-dollar, heart-centred business owner who helps others AND be a present, nurturing, gentle Mum and the cherry on top - a sensual, feminine, caring, doting wife.

The scariest part is, I didn't even realize that I was thinking this until very recently.

Millionaire Mum; The Best of Both Worlds.

A quick disclaimer: At the time of writing and publishing this book, I am not a Millionaire on paper… Yet. However, I am in my head and that's what this book is about. It's a declaration to the universe and to the community that this IS the path for me and what better way to do it then write a book about it?

When I first decided on the name of my book, it made me feel physically ill. My inner voice was scolding me, *"You can't call the book that because you're not a millionaire yet! What will people think?"*

The sick feeling moved up from my tummy into my chest and I started thinking, *"Oh, what if it actually doesn't happen? What if I can't do it? What if I write a book about this and then I don't become a millionaire? I will be ridiculed and rejected!"*

The list was endless.

Debilitating fear, crippling, and utterly mind numbing. Guess what? I did it anyway.

I am going to teach you how to do the same thing. I am well on the way to making my first million but even more importantly, it doesn't really matter because I already feel the connection and abundance on the inside. It radiates from every cell of my being.

Introduction

I discovered the Golden Goose. The connection to myself, my soul purpose aligned with MY values, a way to contribute to the world by being ME. To wake up every morning with purpose and a spring in my step and a sparkle in my eyes. The revelation that everything I desire is within me now and I do not need family, best-seller status or a million dollars as a metric of who I am or my success.

Upon this awareness, my thoughts changed.

Instead of feeling like a fraud I started to ask myself "what else was possible"?

After this awareness, I felt a deep shift and now feel this book and its title has become part of my life's mission. To show you that you can have the best of both worlds and in fact, you already have it NOW.

It starts in your imagination; it starts from inner peace; it starts with gratitude and grace. So, when you do reach your destination, goals, dreams and desires, you'll realise it's not just another empty feeling.

The key is feeling fulfilment. NOW.

I am glad I worked this out because... Guess what? The universe has a way of testing us.

At the time of writing, we are in the year of 2020. Which we all have to know this as the global pandemic of the Coronavirus. You may remember me saying earlier that my husband Gus was an International Airline Pilot for Virgin. Like so many others, we got the phone call every pilot dreads that due to International Travel getting banned, he was stood down.

This time in our lives tested everything we had ever learnt.

We went into lockdown with the rest of the world for three months and were forced to look at the reality of what losing his income meant for our family. More than losing the income, we realised he lost his soul purpose. That man was born to fly.

Every family on the planet has been affected by the global pandemic and I'm sharing our experience and sending so much love to everyone through these times.

The stress and fear of the uncertainty, along with family health issues and new financial burdens put a strain on our relationship with ourselves and each other. This was the shit-hit-the-fan moment for our family.

Watching someone you love lose their life purpose is heartbreaking.

Add home-schooling and a lockdown into the mix and it becomes a pressure cooker. It wasn't long before we both decided to change our perspective. We sat down together and coached each other.

This was the shift we needed.

With love and awareness, we chose a different path. We talked about an official role change where I would step in as the provider and he would be home full-time, while I grew

Introduction

my business which I realised is exactly what people NEED during times of fear and uncertainty.

We used the strategies in my Monthly Mastermind to overcome our challenges. It was a funny feeling logging into my own Online School as a participant and going through the strategies.

I'm pretty proud to say... IT CHANGED OUR LIFE! If you're interested, pop over to my website *www.dianemckendrick. com* to check it out.

We have no idea what will happen in the next few years with so much uncertainty, but what I do know is that we made a declaration that we would work together and do what it takes to get the information that helped us through these times to each other. The world. And now to YOU!

We neutralised loss and grief, dissolved fear, changed our language and built a new plan. We used Focus and Physiology and started meeting every night to discuss how we felt and how we could support and serve each other through this. I declared to Gus that I would use this pain to share what I know with others to help your needs and growth with genuine support.

It's more important to me that you hear and receive the wisdom and gold that has helped me personally, my family and now hundreds of my clients all over the world.

I vowed that I would look back at this experience as a time of reflection and creation. I would find gifts in the tragedy, loss and grief.

This has now become my reality.

In the past several months of the most hectic and chaotic times in our lives (and many others), I:

- Birthed my podcast, *Rise and Shine Podcast Series*, where I have released and published a session every week since it started.

- Quadrupled my business.

- Sold out of my first book and it became an Amazon Best Seller.

- Hosted sold out Women's Empowerment retreats and created an Online Portal for those who couldn't make it due to travel restrictions.

- Moved and transitioned my business online.

- Wrote my second book.

- Published my 2nd Edition Pixie Cards.

- Added a product to my Sterling Silver Remember Ring jewellery line.

- Started extra-support webinars

Was I scared?

Yes.

Introduction

Did people ridicule and attack me?

Yes.

Did I know how?

No.

Did I do it all anyway?

Yes.

Of course, my brain and many people were telling me, *"It's not the right time. No one's got any money. Go sit back in your box…"*

YES! People actually said that to me!

Did I do it all anyway?

HECK YES!

It gifted me a deeper role of compassionate leadership to actually put the people's collective needs ahead of my own.

It's time to stop listening to the nay-sayers and create your own path.

Let's remap the memories with LOVE, together!

Millionaire Mum, The Best of Both Worlds means I get to share my journey and even more powerfully my students and my clients' journeys. I get to witness other men and women stepping into their power and creating a life of abundance and presence doing what they love - with the people they love!

Are you ready to take the leap?

You've come to the right place.

I will guide you through the developmental stages of feeling stuck to being SEEN.

It's like we've got this vortex of collective energy at the moment just rising up and I'm really frothing at the exponential growth, wealth and love that's being completely embraced and embodied by the people right now.

Remember, when it all seems too much, and you don't think you can go on, that's when you're about to leave your comfort zone onto bigger things. When I started, I was completely stuck.

I was craving community, connection, creativity and to be honest, I just didn't know how or where to start.

So, I got a coach (this is your unofficial invitation to reach out!) and I listened, absorbed, and took inspired action. Prior to finding the right coach for me, it seemed I would take two steps forward and five steps back. At the time, I was earning a few hundred dollars a week and working my butt off!

I dearly wanted to create a platform that I could speak from so I could impact more people but I didn't know how to do

Introduction

that because I hadn't done the work. I had not gone through the developmental stages.

In a fast-paced world where so much emphasis is on forward momentum, I find it beneficial to stop for a moment and look how far you have come. My brain is still giving me a hard time for having the courage to claim my million-dollar status before it is real in the physical realm.

Instead of listening to it, I am going to stop for a second and focus on how far I have come.

Let's all do it together now... It was only a little over a year ago that I didn't even have a business bank account. I know!

I had no idea how to invoice someone or the difference between net, gross and revenue. Legit for real!

I met with a fellow entrepreneur for coffee one day (he was a Sales and Marketing Guru) who started asking me questions about my invoicing systems. My net profit vs gross... All I heard was, *"Blah blah blah blah!"*

I had NO IDEA what he was talking about; for me, he may as well have been speaking Italian. I didn't even know the difference between Net and Gross and certainly didn't have any invoicing system...

I had to fess up.

It was a defining moment in my business because I was really far enough along to start taking it seriously, but no one had ever taught me. I fessed up and told him of my zilch business knowledge and as he slowly put his coffee on the table, he looked me right in the eye and asked, *"Diane McKendrick, how on earth have you got this far?!"*

I was embarrassed, ashamed and totally awkward but not because he made me feel that way. He was in total support of guiding, teaching and mentoring me in this part of my business. I had just tried to avoid the yucky feelings, but I knew I needed to feel them in order to make the change.

Honestly, this is where I started, and it's just a little over a year ago. No matter where you are starting with your life and business, best believe there is hope!

I've had so many people support my growth, but it was up to me to say YES.

To be completely honest, you can get all the support in the world, but unless you are ready to receive it and take inspired action, it won't work.

This book will prepare you for the next step in your wholesome life! Choose now what you want!

- Motherhood
- A fit and healthy body
- A booming business
- Flourishing relationships
- Financial freedom

Introduction

You choose. And remember - you can have your cake and eat it, too!

One million dollars a year is only $83k a month. Did you know that?

At the time of writing this book, I have had my first $80k month in business.

Now fast forward to October 2020, at the time of writing this book. In three months, I've already blitzed past that $100k sales in my business!

If the thought of this excites you, this is definitely the book for you.

I am honoured and thrilled to invite you on this absolutely incredible journey, as much as hitting my own goals, I'm also really looking forward to witnessing and watching you annihilate yours.

No more fussing, let's get started.

Now is the time for ACTION.

What I want from you before moving on is a declaration; a statement to anchor you to your commitment to your GREATNESS. A commitment to the oath of having THE BEST OF BOTH WORLDS. A commitment to step out of your comfort zone. To show up. Even when it is scary, even when you don't want to, even when you want to quit.

Declaration

I _____ commit to showing up, sharing, pushing out of my comfort zone, cheering for myself and my sisters and the Collective Community.

_____ (Signature)

Before moving to the next chapter, please take a moment to sign above and join me on social media.

Diane McKendrick: https://www.facebook.com/diane.mckendrick

Those2Sisters Time2Shine: https://www.facebook.com/groups/347312182736084

Instagram: Diane McKendrick

Chapter One

YOUR TIME IS NOW

"It's not about the how, it's about the now."
Diane McKendrick

So, you've just signed the declaration, right? If not, go back and sign it because we are getting straight into it!

My life and business did not start to change until I got honest, until I got a very defined starting point. If you skip this part because it seems too simple (which I know many of you will) you are setting yourself up for a harder journey.

Please do not discount the simple things as I am a master of simplicity and this is one of the reasons for my wholesome success. I do the simple things well. I do the simple things consistently. Individually they don't seem to make much difference, but when you add them up day after day, they provide a lot of deep integrity within your body, soul, business and relationships.

Let's mull over a few questions before we get started. Do you often find yourself:

Aimlessly scrolling Facebook?

Waking up each morning pressing snooze several times?

Struggling to maintain a healthy weight no matter how hard you try?

Fighting with your partner or worse, self-sabotaging potential relationships?

Noticing your finances are like a rollercoaster, never breaking through that invisible ceiling?

Getting up every morning with the empty feeling in your tummy with the voice in your head asking, "Is this all there is?"

I can almost guarantee that regardless of how far are along your journey you are, that you will answer yes to at least one of those questions.

Your Time Is NOW

How do I know? Because I still do them!

I also coach other Millionaire Mums - women much more successful than me and believe me, these ladies have their shit together and many of them will say yes to at least one of the above.

We call it being human.

It is time to stop faffing about and become super clear about your life. Too many of us are living someone else's dream. We wake up each morning on auto-pilot and do what we did the day before. A churning deep pit in your stomach, knowing there is something more for you in life.

You know it is time for a change.

You just don't know how to do it. You don't know where to start. Deeply craving change but not knowing how, where or why to begin.

This is when most coaches will encourage you to set goals, do vision boards, and measure your metrics. Don't get me wrong, that all works but the biggest mistake most of you are making is that you are doing this before you have set your solid foundations. This needs to be done before getting clear on WHERE YOU ARE NOW.

Lucky for you, I have personally been on this journey and taken hundreds of my students through this life-changing information I will be sharing with you in this book.

Let's be honest, I don't have the most conventional approach. In fact, you might find yourself scratching your head asking yourself, *"She wants me to do what?!"*

With that said, I can guarantee that if you find it within you to trust the process and follow my strategies, all areas of your life will transform, and you will wake up - in more ways than one - into your dream life.

Before you set goals, you need a STARTING POINT. Where are you now?

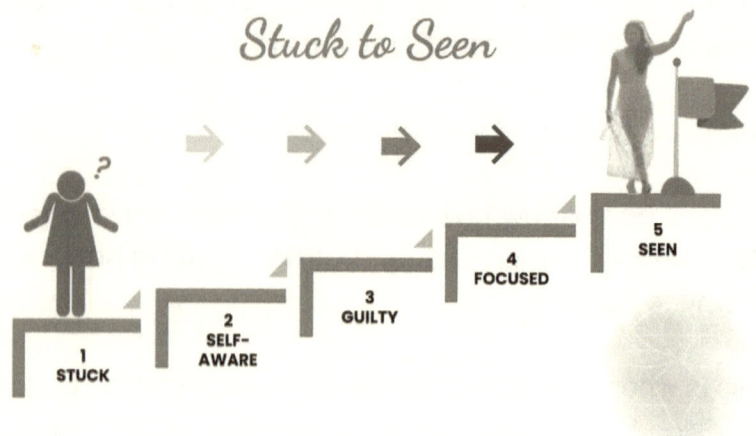

Your Time Is NOW

STUCK

AREAS OF LIFE	DESCRIPTION	SCORE SCORE YOUR SELF FROM A 1-10 1 = TOTALLY NOT ME 10 = I TOTALLY DO THIS
Physique	Usually struggles with weight, often over or underweight. Finds it hard to get out of bed each morning. Hitting snooze.	
Health	Makes unhealthy choices and not a priority.	
Finances	There is never get ahead, paying things off week to week, waiting for pay to come in before paying their bills, always owes money, never gets a head.	
Business/Career	In a 9-5pm job or working shift working, doesn't enjoy it and just does it to pay the bills.	
Home	Cluttered and messy. Tends to be disorganized and there are piles around the house/workspace. 'Can't keep up with housework and always has housework to do.'	
Relationships	Drama. Often arguing or fighting with someone. Strained relationships. Often gossips.	
Thoughts	"I can't be bothered" or "It's too hard" or "No one understands."	

SELF-AWARE

AREAS OF LIFE	DESCRIPTION	SCORE SCORE YOUR SELF FROM A 1-10 1 = TOTALLY NOT ME 10 = I TOTALLY DO THIS
Physique	The body is starting to change as they have implemented a "loose" morning routine. Still struggles to get out of bed but has started to change mindset and internal dialogue.	
Health	It's improving and she's starting to notice how the food she eats feels in her body. Slowly making changes, drinking more water, and starting to feel and look better.	
Finances	She is aware they are not where they need to be. Scared but starting to have conversations and slowly starting to set up systems to help her 'her save and manage money.' Relationship with money is changing.	
Business/Career	Probably still working in a regular day job but daydreaming about the freedom and excitement of the possibility of running her own business.	
Space	Starting to clean out spaces in her house but has basically moved the "stuff" from one pile to another. It's still sitting around the house ready to be moved out but isn't quite ready to let it go yet. Her space is messy but functional.	
Relationships	Starting to notice how she feels when around certain people and doesn't quite have the courage to change peer groups yet but has awareness around how she comes across or how her energy effects others.	
Thoughts	"It seems to work for her, I wonder if I could be/do/have that?" or "Really? I create my own reality?" or "I wonder what else is out there..."	

Millionaire Mum

GUILTY

AREAS OF LIFE	DESCRIPTION	SCORE SCORE YOUR SELF FROM A 1-10 1 = TOTALLY NOT ME 10 = I TOTALLY DO THIS
Physique	Definitely getting stronger and got a good workout routine but starts to feel guilty about the amount of time spent on herself now. If we are not careful here she will spiral back to stuck.	
Health	On the cusp of the upward spiral. The challenge here is that she starts to feel guilty about the extra money being spent on organic food, or clean face care and hair care products.	
Finances	Spending more money on personal development now, and because this developmental stage often coincides with expenditure catching up from the Self aware woman. Waves of guilt wash over her as she watches the expenditure rise and feels sick about having "enough" to pay it all off.	
Business/Career	She's caught herself chastising herself and saying, "I'm stupid for even thinking that could happen to me. Let me know to stay in my 9-5 job lane. It's all too much".	
Relationships	Avoids connection with people as she starts to question her own authenticity. Experiences "Imposter Syndrome.".	
Thoughts	"I don't deserve it" or "When will this come crashing down?"	

FOCUS

AREAS OF LIFE	DESCRIPTION	SCORE SCORE YOUR SELF FROM A 1-10 1 = TOTALLY NOT ME 10 = I TOTALLY DO THIS
Physique	She is starting to get strong, fit and healthy. A solid morning routine which is non compromisable. Early to rise. Does the early morning obnoxious FB live as the masses "roll out of bed" or press snooze. Positive internal dialogue speaking and coaching herself through the challenges. Has an exercise routine in place.	
Health	Health is on an upward spiral. Eating well, drinking plenty of water. Consistent and often over the top. Not listening to her body as much and we need to be careful here of burnout. Overachieving tendencies.	
Finances	Has a lot more as she is doing more, working really hard, working out really hard, networking like a ninja but still juggling finances as she has more but is spending more. She has experienced waves of abundance and is now working REALLY HARD for more.	
Business/Career	Starting her own heart-centered, wholesome business and working super hard at it. Also, It is here she needs to be careful as other areas of her life can be affected by the time, effort, and energy she's putting into her business. She's working hard, pushing boundaries instead of setting them, and it's FAST. She tries to do everything herself, not having time or trust to train staff.	
Relationships	A lot healthier but can be strained as she navigates the next level of her business. Most people around here don't understand her drive and focus and she can sometimes feel outcast. She no longer has time for gossip and if she catches herself gossiping, she'll chastise herself because she knows better.	
Thoughts	"How can I fit more ?"	

Your Time Is NOW

SEEN

AREAS OF LIFE	DESCRIPTION	SCORE SCORE YOUR SELF FROM A 1-10 1 = TOTALLY NOT ME 10 = I TOTALLY DO THIS
Physique	Strong, fit and healthy. Combining strength with flexibliy as she knows both are important. A well rounded approach with a deep understanding of what her body needs daily. Wakes up with out an alarm alert and ready for her day of service.	
Health	In great health as she maintains a beautiful balance of tuning in and being present with her thoughts, urges, impulses and how to neutralise them.	
Finances	She is in an abundance mindset and is free from the competition and rat race. A deep knowing Abundance is her birthright and the physical realm reflects that.	
Business/Career	This woman manages and organises her time wisely. She sets clear boundaries in her personal life and business and by some miracle has time to fit it ALL in. She is disciplined with her calendar. She is clear and committed to her current nurturing funnel. She is efficient and effective communicator, with herself and others. Creates enormous income by doing what she loves with people she loves. She is living her Soul Purpose and helping others live theirs. She receives openly and has started to outsource the work giving her even more time to spend with her family, health, holidaying or what ever fills her back up .	
Relationships	Harmonious and connected relationships. She spends a lot of time by herself. Feels safe to express and have loving, difficult conversations.	
Thoughts	*"How can I help more people?"*	

When you read through the above table, mark on Diagram 1 which developmental stage you are in at the moment. You may notice you are a combination of a few. However, you will be dominant in one and resonate mostly with one of the stages.

Once you uncover your starting point, we can help guide you through the developmental stages of the important areas of your life.

We are now able to break down the areas of life and give them a score to get even more CLARITY about where you are right now.

Millionaire Mum

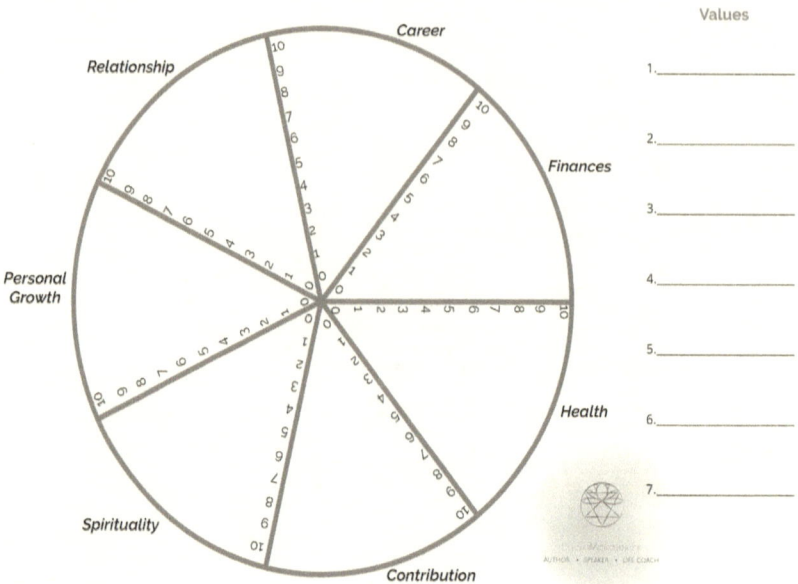

This Wheel of Life is broken up into several main areas of your life. Work your way around the wheel and score each area of your life. 0 being *"Dismal, needs improvement"* and 10 being *"The best it can get."*

Here is an example copy:

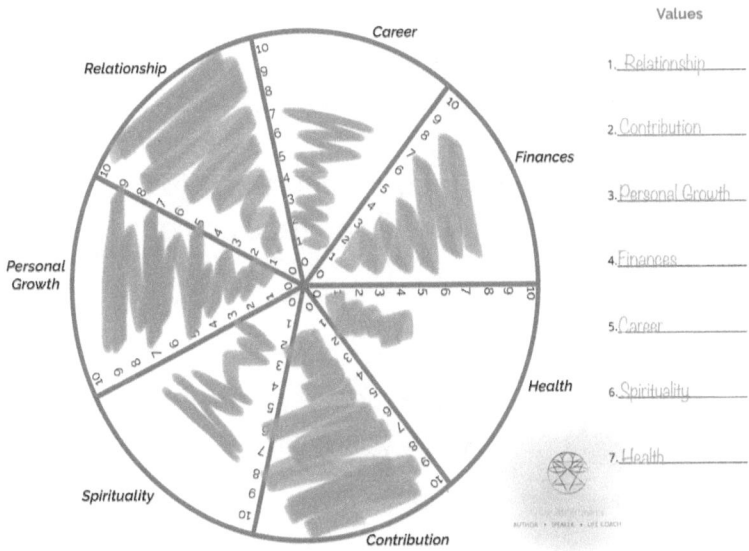

For your digital copy of the wheel, please visit
www.dianemckendrick.com/wheeloflife

I've noticed most people don't have a starting point. Some know what they want (somewhat) and others have no idea, and most dismiss the starting point altogether. Some can become overly focused on the goal, the dream, the fantasy.

Using your time now to do the Wheel of Life exercise is so powerful.

Just like a map, if you do not have a starting point, how do you know which way to go towards your destination?

I adore it when my students come to me with their very first Wheel of Life. To visually see and feel how far they have come is fulfilling.

The self-development industry (myself included) can be overly focused on "overachieving" and "forward momentum" that we forget how far we have come. It's always nice to stop for a moment and honour how far you have come.

In fact, do it now!

Take a moment to rewind the memory bank back five or ten years and notice how much you have grown, how far you have come.

Celebrate yourself.

This is training ourselves to honour our growth instead of having an obnoxious, insatiable, empty drive for more, more, more!

Once you have completed the Wheel of Life, you may notice there is some work to do in your life. A nice plump wheel will flow and move with ease, although often when we complete our wheel for the first time, it resembles something more of a starfish.

When I did my first one, I was so disheartened as it looked more like a mangled starfish than any kind of wheel. Mine consisted of mainly 2's and 3's with maybe a 5 being my highest.

Dismal.

It upset me. Made me uncomfortable. Gave me the reality check I needed in order to make some changes. You might be having a reality check now…

It is at this point I mention, *"Do not soften it. Do not tell yourself it's not that bad."*

Immerse yourself in the pain of years of not looking after yourself, years of listening to your limiting beliefs, years of playing it small, years of putting rubbish into your body, years of abusing your body, mind and soul.

Feel the discomfort. NOW.

Even if you are not uncomfortable with it, trick your brain momentarily for the purpose of the exercise. Let yourself be disgusted for a moment.

Stop using "softeners" and lying to yourself. As humans, we do it ALL the time and it makes us feel better, but it does not serve us. Change occurs in one of two circumstances:

1. A move towards pleasure.
2. A move away from pain.

Which would make you move faster with more intensity?

Which would inspire you or scare you into taking action immediately?

1. Taking action towards having a fit, healthy, strong body. e.g. Starting your morning routine, eating better, and cutting alcohol because you know it's good for you and it feels good.

OR

2. If the doctor said to you, *"You are sick, you will die in two weeks if you don't start looking after yourself. You need to start a morning routine, eat better, cut alcohol. Your life depends on it."*

Which option would have you take more intense and immediate action?

The PAINFUL circumstance.

It is the way our brain is wired so work with me while we stop with the softeners and the it's-not-that-bad's and we really go deep into the worst-case scenario if you don't make the changes you need to make in your life.

Now is not the time for fluffy, positive affirmations.

Now is the time to go deep and feel the pain.

I use this process regularly with all areas of my life. I simulate the worst-case scenario and let myself believe it for a little while. It sure does get my butt into ACTION in making the necessary changes to upgrade and up level all areas of my life.

We take our students through this process at our 3-Day Soul Mastery Retreat. If you want more information or to attend the retreat and have me take you through the process personally, visit *www.those2sisters.com/retreats/*

This is only the part one of the process.

Once you get clear about your starting point and be brutally honest with it (an experience most won't have the courage to do), you will be one step closer to having it ALL. To living the life, you deserve and desire.

Part two of the process is one that many people miss or do in the wrong order. They hope and pray, take minimal action and then wonder why it never happens for them.

It's because they don't really know what they want. The majority of us have been wired to focus on the problem and what we don't want, rather than what we do want.

Our brain simply does not recognise the word "not."

For example, if I say to you, *"Don't think of a big, green elephant. Don't think of a big, green elephant. Whatever you do, don't think of a big, green elephant!"*

What are you thinking of?

Let me guess, you're thinking of a big green elephant? Simply by trying not to.

Your brain does not recognise the word 'don't.' It only hears the command which in this case is, *"Think of a big green elephant."*

Take a moment now to write down the things you do not want and then change the language to what you do want.

WHAT DO YOU REALLY WANT?

DON'T WANT	DO WANT
EXAMPLE	EXAMPLE
TIRED	ENERGY
BROKE	ABUNDANCE
LONELY	CONNECTION
OVERWHELMED	PEACEFUL
YOUR TURN	YOUR TURN

Now you have a Starting Point and you have clarity around what you want, it's time for me to let you in on a little, life-changing secret. I use this manifesting trick in all areas of my life.

You may have even heard me talk about it on a podcast or FB live. It is so simple that once again, it often gets overlooked by many people.

Are you ready for the top-secret information that is going to change your life?

Here goes...

Your brain doesn't know the difference between something vividly imagined and an actual memory.

Therefore, when you were eating breakfast this morning (which probably happened in real time) or you're actually picking up this book to read (which if you are reading this definitely happened in real time), these are examples of an actual memory of things that have happened in real time in your life.

It is the same to your brain as your wildest dreams and fantasies that have not occurred in real time, yet. The only reason your brain can tell the difference is because of the emotion we choose to put with it, consciously or subconsciously as a human.

Drum roll please... This information is MIND BLOWING! Literally!

Okay, I understand. The above is a bit of a mouthful and mind bend to comprehend and a few of you may be thinking, *"Okay Diane, let's get this straight. Are you telling me that my brain can't tell the difference between me really eating breakfast, or picking this book up and reading it and all my wildest craziest dreams and desires?"*

Yep, that's exactly what I am telling you!

Essentially, it's quantum physics. We literally trick our own brain into believing it is already true. Once you do the visualisation, add all of your senses and feel it. It is as good as done in your brain. Combine this with emotion and repetition and it simply HAS to happen.

The RAS (Reticular Activating System) switches on and searches for conversations, interactions, opportunities, circumstances, and situations to make it true.

Just like the yellow car exercise. How many yellow cars have you seen in the last week? You probably can't remember seeing any, right? Now that I tell you to look for them and count them, report back to me and tell me how many you see? I guarantee you will see loads of them.

Were they there before? Of course, they were there! You just didn't see them because you RAS wasn't switched on or primed to see them. It is now.

Every time you see a yellow car, I want you to call out *"Spotto!"* This was a family game we play in the car when we are on holidays. The word *"spotto"* is anchored to the depth and possibility of life.

It reminds me of what is possible and to start with IMAGINATION. That everything we seek is already there, waiting for us.

We just need to match the vibrations to see it.

I have just explained the process I am personally using in the approach to this book and my million-dollar business. To my brain, it's as good as DONE. Now, it is only a matter of real time catching up.

The power of manifestation is real.

With this new knowledge, I want to help you magnify and amplify the certainty of the thing that you desire and the magic you're calling into your life. Remind each and every one of you that you can have ALL THE THINGS!

It starts with knowing where you are NOW without sugar coating it, changing your language and getting clear about what you want and IMAGINING it as though it is happening to you now. Literally waking up every morning and cultivating the feelings and emotions of YOUR dream.

Now we have that clear, you can see that it's actually fairly straightforward. So, let's take it a step further. I am committed to making this absolute for you and a bullet proof way to live the life of your dreams.

Let's take a moment to visit the things that you said you want in life. Often in my workshops or at my Soul Mastery Retreats when we do our "Vision Board with a Twist," many people tell me about the things they desire.

The tangible assets that make our life full, luxurious, fun and fulfilling. The things that most people think when they acquire, they will be happy.

I recently noticed that when I look at most people's vision boards (before they work with me), they are full of the things that people think will make them happy, such as:

- Hot beach body
- New fancy cars
- Amazing houses on the seaside or in the French Alps
- A handsome man or woman as their new life partner
- A boat
- A caravan
- Healthy, colourful meals
- Organic food
- Lots of money
- Holidays

What would your vision board look like?

Close your eyes now and imagine it.

Here is the magic question and why my vision boards work and don't just get put on the wall to look good and inspire. My Vision Board with a Twist is a practical and powerful way to get your vision board on steroids!

*What is the **feeling** that thing on your board will provide for you?*

Example: If you are manifesting a new car, is FREEDOM the feeling it will bring you?

Maybe independence? Perhaps something else?

What about the hot beach body? Is it confidence and health that would be the feeling it would give you?

A new house? Maybe security and belonging?

If we know our starting point, we can change our language, imagine having it all AND cultivate and nourish the FEELING that the tangible things will give you. With this knowledge, you will be 99% ahead of the rest.

This is literally the process I have used to create my dream life and the steps I am following to becoming a millionaire in real time.

At this risk of sounding cliché, it really is all in the mind. It starts inside first, and we create it step by step.

I prefer this fulfilled and feeling method of Goal Setting and magnetising your dreams, as the old paradigm for me was fairly grim. Either I got to the goal and said, *"Great, what's next?"* which launched me into a never-ending cycle of, *"Not enough, never enough."*

I would hit one goal and then dismiss it and say, *"But, what's next?"*

Much like the time when I won a gold medal at the National School Girl Titles for swimming; I felt good for a week and then empty again, chasing the next ego high. Alternatively, I was miles away from my goal and was left feeling useless and hopeless. Neither very attractive nor resourceful options.

Millionaire Mum

Add a conscious, connected community to your goals, dreams and desires and you can pretty much sit back and watch the magical fireworks display.

Life as you know it will never be the same.

Your turn:

THE FEELING THE "THING" GIVES ME

THING	FEELING
EXAMPLE	EXAMPLE
CAR	FREEDOM, INDEPENDENCE
BEACH BODY	CONFIDENCE, HEALTH
NEW HOUSE	SECURITY
YOUR TURN	YOUR TURN
_____	_____
_____	_____
_____	_____

SUMMARY:

- Most people don't have a starting point. They soften the reality of where they are right now by telling themselves it's not that bad.

- By not wanting something, you are attracting it to yourself.

- Change your focus to what you do WANT.

- You will most likely make a change if your brain perceives discomfort or danger, so we can simulate that internally to avoid having to really go there and get stuck.

- When doing vision boards or goal setting, it's crucial to uncover the "feeling" you think the tangible thing will give you and cultivate that.

- Change your internal language; change your outcome.

- Yellow cars do exist, you just haven't seen them. Because you haven't been looking.

Chapter Two

FINDING THE GENIUS WITHIN

"Be the beam of light; the lantern that lights the path for those around you."
Diane McKendrick

I'm going to ask you a question right now that will absolutely change the trajectory of your life.

We ask this at our half day workshop, The Six Steps to Soul Success. The majority of people struggle with this and it's often one of the most profound ah-ha moments shared within the group. So, the question is:

Who are you?

If you can't introduce yourself by saying your name, your age, your job, the fact that you're a parent, what you do for a living, the fact that you're married or have a partner, who are you? By taking away all the labels, all the things that you have been told that you are by society, the labels and the identity... Who are you?

_____

_____

_____

We are taught from a very young age to search outside of ourselves for our identity. When introducing ourselves or answering who we are, most of us instinctively respond with our roles, job, and accomplishments whilst searching externally for the answer.

When we do this in our workshops, initially, there is an awkward silence as people shift uncomfortably in their seats. Holding space as each person accesses something deeper than what they have been taught, I cultivate the awkwardness for a little longer.

Side note: If you are wanting to become a coach of any sort, get used to awkward silence. This is where the magic happens.

Just after long enough, I start hearing words like:

- LOVE
- LIGHT
- COURAGE
- STRENGTH
- HEALER
- COMPASSION
- POWERFUL
- NURTURER
- SUNSHINE
- ENERGY

The awkward silence subsides, and it's replaced with a buzz of possibility and awakening.

The energy in the room is renewed and people get the spark back in their eyes. It's so powerful in fact, that in most workshops, at least someone is moved to tears as they reconnect back to their higher self.

So, let's do it now. Strip back all the layers. Let go of everything that you have ever been taught about yourself and GO DEEPER.

Who are you without all the stuff?

_____

_____

_____

Take all the time you need and fill the above space with as much love, light and energy as you can… And then ADD MORE!

I remember being horrified when my coach asked me this question 20 years ago.

She was really good at awkward silences and staring at me for nearly 45 minutes as I peeled back all the layers. I had NO IDEA who I was but had created a whole identity and story to support what I thought I "should" be telling people. At the time, the only things I could initially answer were, *"My name is Diane. I am an athlete, I work here and I do this, I do that, blah, blah blah…"*

It is shocking how such a simple question can have such a deep impact on someone.

It was before I had done any personal development and I was uncomfortable. Squirming in my seat, having a full physiological effect and feeling physically ill with the shock as I felt extremely vulnerable. As I took the time to feel the feelings, it was like the whole process worked through my body.

So, you may be wondering... How can I infuse this into my life now when meeting new people? How this would be received if I walk up to a Mum in the schoolyard and say, *"Hi there, I am love, light and energy."*

It's possible she might give you a strange look and walk the other way.

Likewise, if you're at a networking event and wander up to someone to give them one of your million dollar smiles and say, *"Hi, I am courage, strength and passion."*

You may be left to eat dinner or have your glass of wine on your own and not invited to any more events.

Let's be clear, I am not advocating this!

Side note: If you did this at one of my events, you would likely be embraced in a bear hug and celebrated! Let's keep in mind the rest of society isn't always as committed to growth and development as we are, right?

My invitation to you is that when someone asks you what you do and who you are, you will answer in the conventional, culturally correct and safe way. For example, I would say, *"My name is Diane McKendrick, and I'm a life coach, best-selling author and public speaker. I'm also a mother of two, a million-dollar business owner and I'm a loving, doting wife."*

Instead of bringing the energy or hiding behind my business, kids or accomplishments - which I have done in the past and probably many of you also do - let's bring the essence and energy of the words we chose above. So, the words we say and the things we do are infused with the essence and energy of LOVE, LIGHT, ENERGY, COURAGE, and COMPASSION.

If you can do this, you will be mesmerising.

People will be magnetised to you and they won't know why. It's because you FEEL GOOD, not only to them but most importantly, to YOURSELF.

I get this feedback regularly, *"Di, how do you do it? We feel you coming before we see you? When you walk into a room, it is like you are a magnet and people are drawn to you and mesmerised by your presence. What is your secret?"*

When you fully own all of your traits and acknowledge all parts of yourself, the full spectrum woman, when you dig deeper and peel back the layers it's mesmerising, magnetising and contagious.

This is my invitation to you:

Be this beam of light; the lantern that lights the path for those around you.

What if people meeting you don't like the light? What if your gorgeous, soulful and divine presence repulses them? Well, that is okay, too! As with everything, there are always two sides to the coin. This is where we discover the difference between self-esteem and self-worth.

Self-esteem is embracing the concept of the LIGHT.

Accepting all the magnificent things about yourself. This is the part where traditional personal development lets us down.

To experience and live from a place of true self-worth, you need to be able to accept the polar opposites of yourself. The perceived good and the perceived bad.

As humans, we have made it a habit to attach to one side of the polarity. Either, the good or the bad. Good or bad is only a perception, anyway. Good or bad compared to what?

What most of us do is then only accept and share the perceived positive traits. Especially in the social media world. We attach to the perceived positive and resist the perceived negative by not accepting the lazy, unmotivated, boring parts of ourselves.

As per the diagram below, it helps take many people on the journey from low self-esteem, believing they are lazy, unmotivated, boring, fearful to high self-esteem.

When you are attached to low self-esteem, your life is full of shame and guilt. When you attach to the other side of the coin, you are in pride and each can be as detrimental as the other.

The Magic Key is the synthesis of both the high and low self-esteem which will give you full SELF-WORTH; living from a place of truth and presence.

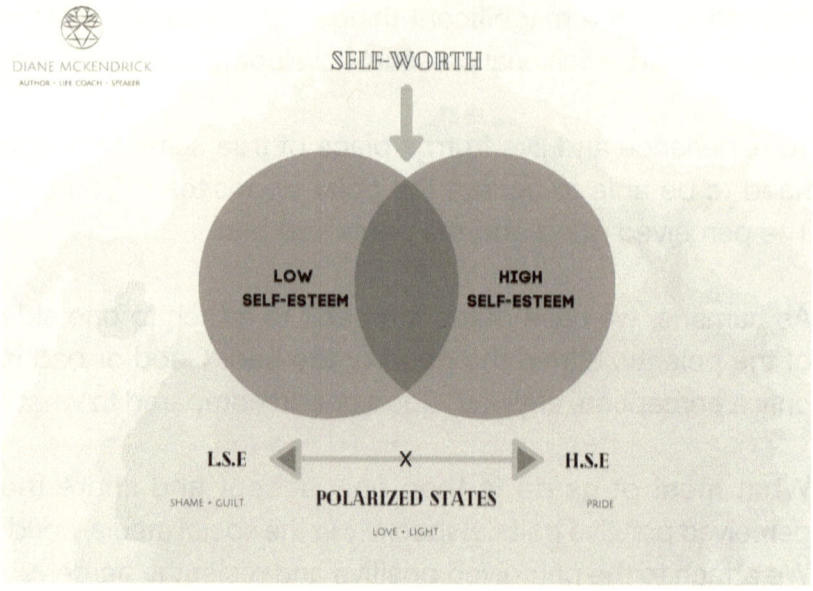

Let's stop attaching to the labels and feel and understand that we are FULL SPECTRUM.

As much as we are activated, we are also lazy; as much as we are honest, we are dishonest; as much as we are courageous, we are fearful. A deep understanding and commitment to living your life by this principle will create so much deep connection, awareness and freedom.

If you would like to research more into this topic pop over to *Apple iTunes* or *Spotify* and listen to my Podcast from the *Rise and Shine Podcast Series*, which is called "Self Esteem vs Self Worth."

Once you embrace this way of living and own all of your traits, life transforms before your very eyes. Literally with the click of your fingers!

Now that we have discovered that we are ALL the things, it might be time for me to bring up that for many years, I thought I was going crazy because I heard voices.

Yep, that's right, there were voices in my head! Many, many, many voices! Like an orchestra so loud telling me all sorts of things, giving me random advice, chastising me, scolding me, ridiculing me. Sometimes the voices told me nice things, but not very often and the loudest voices were definitely the one that constantly told me:

"You're not good enough."

"You don't know how."

"You're an idiot."

"Why did you say that?"

And many other critical, scolding things they would say to me.

I used to try and completely override the voice and guess what? It didn't work.

I've since learnt that it is the ego and it is there to keep me safe. It is our two-million-year-old reptile brain talking, which is simply wired for survival. Its job is to keep us in our box as it thinks we are safe there.

Instead of trying to dismiss it or get rid of it, fight against it, I decided to do the same as I did in the self-worth strategy…

I decided to ACCEPT it. To be grateful for it. To honour it.

To give the voice that used to have so much power over me a name. So, I named it and yep, you guessed it - IT STARTED TO TALK BACK! Yes! You heard me right! I both named and gave my ego a voice and it talked back to me.

My ego's name is Digsy and the conversation with her goes a little like this:

"Digsy, firstly, thank you. Thank you for trying to keep me safe and doing your job. You have been loyal and diligent in keeping me safe. I am now at a point in my life where you can have a rest and relax. Let me take over, I now command you that if it isn't a life and death situation, you are NOT required. You have been driving my car of life and now you can move over to the passenger seat and take a break."

At this point in the visualisation and conversation, the ego is now in the passenger seat, which leaves space in the front seat for your HIGHER SELF to start to drive your car (a metaphor for directing YOUR LIFE).

Occasionally, I'll start to hear snide remarks from the passenger seat, Digsy is rebelling:

"You will never make it. You don't know the way. You're hopeless. Why bother you know you will fail anyway?"

I notice the voice has less control over me now, it feels less overwhelming, and further away as it has been in the past. The voice has less force, less control over me, it's not as loud, actually. Now, it is barely a whisper. I can still hear her, though. Once again, I say,

"Digsy, firstly, thank you. Thank you for trying to keep me safe and doing your job. You have been loyal and diligent in keeping me safe. I am now at a point in my life where you can have a rest and relax. Let me take over, I now command you that if it isn't a life and death situation, you are NOT required. You have been driving my car of life and now you can move over to the passenger seat and take a break."

I can barely hear her anymore which gives my HIGHER SELF (who I have named Diana) permission to DRIVE the car of my life.

Together as a whole, we take on the journey of life.

Every now and again, I will notice that Digsy has snuck her way back into the front seat and I have to go through the above visualisation and dialogue to remove her from the driver's seat.

When Digsy is in the driver's seat, life is chaotic, dramatic, painful and challenging. When Diana is in charge, everything flows, momentum picks up and things seem to fall into place easily and effortlessly.

Now it's your turn, pick a name for your ego and one for your higher self.

Ego Name: _____

Higher Self Name: _____

The perfectionists amongst have kept reading and skipped writing the names above because you can't think of a suitable name. You, yes YOU! Stop reading now and put two names above. The name does not matter, the action does!

Do not be fooled, if you still do not have the names your ego is still driving! Pick a name, any name and WRITE IT ABOVE. And direct her to the back seat, baby!

DO IT NOW.

To ensure you don't have any excuses not to complete the above, here is a list of 10 names my current clients use. Pick one of each and stick with it:

EXAMPLES:

EGO NAME	HIGHER SELF
1. Missy	Michelle
2. Barry	Lisa
3. Cheryl	Bec Sta
4. Nancy	Jody
5. Cindy	Natasha
6. Deborah	Karen
7. Barbara	Caroline
8. Grizelda	Bronwyn
9. Louise	Sharon
10. Megan	Bryony

Finding The Genius Within

Now that you have picked a name, please go over to *Diane Mckendrick* on Facebook and share your ego name! I will be watching for who takes action and is ready to change their life.

Hint: I give prizes to action takers!

The ego is clever, and it has adapted and by the time you hit SEEN status within the developmental stage, you will notice it has also grown and evolved to actually disguise itself as your higher self!

So, when you work with me one on one in the packages, or at the retreats, we go through a process to dissolve this. The process is too extensive to share in one book. I wanted to alert you to this tricky little adaptation as you might meet it before your chance to come along to a retreat and I want to make sure you are ready for it!

If you don't recognise it and acknowledge it, it's a quick slide back down the ladder to STUCK.

The process is designed to help you pinpoint the messages and the downloads coming through from your ego that is now in disguise as your higher self.

The ego is extremely clever, and it's evolved with you.

You may start to notice it is more challenging to distinguish between the voice of the ego or the higher self.

Because you have been doing so much work on yourself. Like reading this book, listening to my *Rise and Shine Podcast Series*, tuning in to the *Weekly Wisdom Webinars*, possibly attending my exclusive events, hopefully lucky enough to attend one my retreats and being immersed in a conscious, creative and supportive community, your internal growth will be rapid, sustainable and empowering.

Each area of your life will have improved health, wealth, relationships and career. A fully wholesome approach.

Now, more than ever, you have to watch for the ego disguising itself as the higher self. Remember it has spent a large portion of the last amount of time sitting in the back seat observing and learning EVERY MOVE of your higher self.

I observe this regularly with myself and my clients who are about to take a massive leap in their life. Often this is relevant and present in a time of monumental growth.

Think about how you feel when you have been offered an amazing opportunity. Something that puts you out of your comfort zone, something beyond your current financial thermostat, something unfamiliar but exciting to your central nervous system. I've watched as many of my clients go through this when committing to my high-end packages. Their heart and higher self say, *"YES."*

Full stop.

It is a new time and financial commitment, so they go away to think about it.

Their ego says:

"How are you going to afford that?"

"You don't deserve it."

"The last time you bought a course you didn't do it."

"Don't spend that money on yourself, the family needs it more."

"You won't have time."

"You never follow through."

"Don't be stupid."

They go away, think about it and a few will take the leap and say YES! Sign up, make it happen and EVERY AREA OF THEIR LIFE BLOSSOMS AND BLOOMS. I call these people, *"The Masters of Their Life."*

Others come back after thinking about it, using language like:

"It's not in alignment for me right now."

"I sat with this for a while."

"I pulled the card and it told me it's not the right time."

Sometimes, that's their truth, however my observation is that often, it is our ego disguising itself as higher self. I ask myself, *"What will my life be like a year from now if I DON'T do this?"*

I listen to the answer and once again, it confirms what my heart already knew.

Mainly it's just my brain and ego working out logistics, finances, and time but what I have worked out in my years of personal development and coaching is that if I don't say yes and create the space; NOTHING WILL CHANGE.

If I feel the full body yes in my heart, I say YES before I am ready. I say YES because I feel it in my body.

I say YES because I deserve it.

It works both ways. Sometimes it will be a full body NO. You may have some suave business person talking you into a YES. I have also had this happen to me many times and had to set a boundary and say NO and mean it!

Always remember "insert ego name here" is part of who you are and they are there to protect you. Remember she is a small child ready to manipulate, negotiate and adapt to get what she wants. Speak to her as you would a small child, and if she is being overly opinionated and unruly like Digsy, then repeat your Higher Self exercise and quieten her.

Another technique I use and can share with you is uncovering what your ego likes to do. How she relaxes. Some like playing with puppies, some like watching tv - I know that Digsy likes to sleep. It used to be alcohol and partying she liked but now it's sleep. She likes to sleep and eat chips.

Once you uncover what it is your ego likes to do, you can give her permission to go do that!

If you didn't think I was crazy before, you definitely will now! Hahaha!

So, my internal dialogue goes something like this, *"Thanks Digsy. Go have a sleep and eat some chips. Come back when you're done, and I'll be here ready and waiting for you."*

Digsy goes for a sleep which keeps her quiet while Diana and I come into the office and WRITE and CREATE! Diana is thriving, and I froth at the magic we create together in the next few hours together!

Hold on a sec. I'm nearly finished with this chapter and all of a sudden, I'm thinking, maybe I have been questioning the name of this book because:

"It's not the right time?"

"Maybe I'm out of alignment?"

"Perhaps I should pick a safer topic?"

Tell me, is this the disguised ego or higher self talking?!

So, Digsy got all cute and clever and snuck back from her sleep just to get her last few messages heard!

Millionaire Mum

And again... I put her in the back seat, back to bed, send her to play out on the beach or whatever her heart desires so Diana and I can get back to business.

SUMMARY

- You are more than you name, your age, or your job. Many people identify with themselves by what they do.

- Know you know you are so much more and will take the essence of love, light, and energy into each interaction. You will become mesmerising and magnetic.

- Some people won't like you and that is okay. You are FULL SPECTRUM and full self-worth is the synthesis of low self-esteem and high self-esteem. When you own ALL of your traits and stop attaching to one side e.g. positive.

- You will have FULL SELF WORTH. It is unshakeable.

- Ego is important and is designed to protect us, subconsciously, it has been driving many of us for too long. It's time to stop listening to it blindly, resisting it and letting it drive your life.

- You will have a better relationship with it if you name it and open a dialogue with it.

- Acknowledge your ego, thank it and demand it is only required if it's a life or death situation. Mostly, it's NOT!

- Use it when it is helpful and put it in the back seat or to sleep if it is not!

- Always remember that the ego can disguise itself as the higher self. Be mindful of this.

Chapter Three

"X" MARKS THE SPOT - SOUL PURPOSE

*"A person who wakes up on purpose,
is a happy person."
Diane McKendrick*

It is my intention that by the end of this chapter you are closer than you have ever been to discovering your SOUL PURPOSE.

Your purpose is here and now, you're closer to your purpose than what you think.

This is going to be one of the most earth-shattering discoveries of your life. When you discover what you are on this earth for… EVERYTHING CHANGES.

SOUL PURPOSE is a specific calling from your soul.

I remember in my younger years feeling completely empty and lost, constantly striving and looking on the outside of myself for validation. Often feeling exhausted, fatigued, scattered and lonely. On autopilot, day after day after day. Doing the same monotonous things.

I didn't question it, heck, I barely knew I was unhappy because almost everyone around me was living a similar life.

Every now and again I would meet a person who felt different. I noticed their energy, their sparkle, their zest for life and general enthusiasm towards life. It seemed everything they touched turned to gold.

I wanted to know how.

The difference between these people and the masses (and myself at the time) is that they had discovered and were living their Soul Purpose. Finding your Soul Purpose is the starting point to the mastery of your life.

"X" Marks the Spot - Soul Purpose

Your purpose is unique to you and it's not the same as anyone else. It is here and now and you are much closer to it than you think.

I met one of these sparkly, zesty beings (also known as rainbow unicorns) one day. I was intrigued. I thought, if he can do it, well so can I!

I became an investigator asking LOTS of questions. Quizzing him on everything from his morning routine, sleep patterns, having an insightful and profound conversation as he generously shared some of his secrets with me and now I want to share them with you!

Firstly, he reminded me how we are a soul, mind and body. He broke down the whole concept into understandable terms which was easy for me to grasp and therefore I'm able to relay it to you!

Our soul's role is to indicate desires.

Our mind chooses between the desires.

Our body enacts that choice.

Not rocket science, hey?

When he explained it to me in this way, it was easy to digest. He went on to explain that our physical reality is already being subtly guided by our soul's desires, though we may not see it. Many of us do not see it as we have not been shown how to notice it.

Imagine your soul guided desires as scattered, confusing dots on a dot-to-dot picture. Before connecting the lines, it's a confusing mess. There is no structure, no outline, no order. Just a confusing scattered mess. Kind of what my life used to feel - with no order and no organisation.

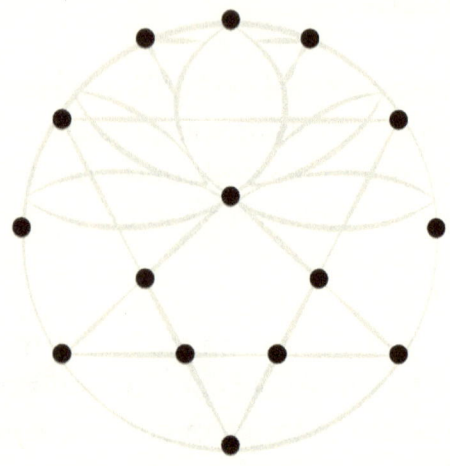

Most people, unless they have done this type of work are scattered of mind and unsure of their true purpose. The dots from your dot-to-dot drawing have disintegrated and faded. They've become confusing, messy, scattered, and out of order.

Those of us who commit to mastery and empowering our lives, have an ordered mind with clarity of our true Soul Purpose. These little black dots on the messy dot-to-dot picture are refined, integrated and skilfully arranged into a beautiful piece of work of art.

"X" Marks the Spot - Soul Purpose

The art work (or picture) represents your life, your SOUL PURPOSE. The picture is CLEAR and the **expression** and **fulfillment** of these soul guided desires is YOUR PURPOSE.

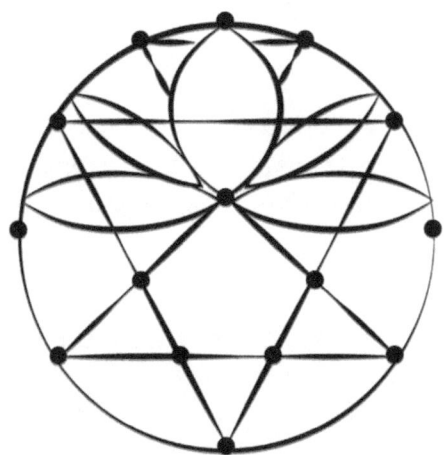

Once you have joined your dots and your Purpose Picture becomes clear, pluck out the BIG DOTS. Visit these dots and refine them. Rise them, polish them make them sparkly and clear to luminate the path.

The empowerment, fulfilment and health you achieve in life is directly proportional to how intensely you pursue your purpose, over other paths that life will throw in your way.

Most people won't take the time out to listen to their soul's desires.

Unfortunately, because of the way society is in the 21st century, only a few of us will discover it and even less will choose to live it.

I guarantee when you are around a person who has discovered and living their purpose, you will feel it. It emanates from them. We all know people like this. Instead of being jealous, comparing or getting tall poppy syndrome, try asking some quality questions and absorbing their wisdom and zest for life.

When you personally uncover yours, it will transform every area of your life in the most life-altering way. Recognising or acknowledging others living their Soul Purpose is one of the first steps of living yours.

The common misconceptions or myths out there about Soul Purpose is that:

   A. It is on the outside of you.
   B. You are moving toward it.

A: Most people think their Soul Purpose is on the outside of them. Something to do or say, accomplish or have. An example of this is when a mother believes that her children are her Soul Purpose. Your children are not your Soul Purpose.

The truth is that YOU HAVE IT IN YOU. NOW.

At this very moment, it can't be seen, held or moulded. But it is there, waiting patiently for you to connect to it. Most of us are taught to ignore it, stifle it and simply not pay it any attention. A lot of the western culture ideals are responsible for us adding many layers, expectations, and limiting beliefs when it comes to meeting and greeting our soul's desires.

"X" Marks the Spot - Soul Purpose

I've watched dozens of people spending so much time, effort and energy searching for it. Looking in all the wrong places. Some areas I have noticed where people waste a lot of time searching include their:

- Relationships
- Bank Accounts
- Cars
- Job
- Shopping
- Kids

B: Many people think their goals are their Soul Purpose. Something in the future that you are moving towards. That is your destiny, dreams or desires. Your Soul Purpose is not in the future. It is in the PRESENT with you right now. Many people are so distracted by being busy or organising their life and get their goals, dreams and desires, they negate the POWER of the NOW.

Always striving. Rarely listening.

Another distraction to watch out for, which will keep you from your Soul Purpose is when life gets hard (which it will). Your brain will want to disassociate to your current, present path and fantasise to something else. A good way to notice if you are doing this is if you are thinking, *"I'll be happy when..."* or comparing to someone else's life and thinking, *"They have got it all!"*

The key here is GRATITUDE for the PRESENT moment. Even if it's hard, be honest, do the work and sit with the discomfort so you can emerge with deep wisdom and connection to yourself that many don't have the courage to undertake.

Your Soul Purpose is NOW. Whatever you are doing RIGHT NOW is part of your Soul Purpose.

The process I take my students through in my Monthly Mastermind helps you join the dots to create your Masterpiece. To access the Soul Purpose Process in my Monthly Mastermind, visit www.dianemckendrick.com

One dot by itself doesn't mean much, or a whole lot of messy, seemingly misplaced dots without order and no structure, with a little love and attention will transform into your greatest piece of art. Before doing my Purpose Process and gaining this awareness, your Soul Purpose picture may well look like a massive mess of black dots all over the page.

Once the dots are joined, you can clearly see the picture. Once you see the picture you can colour it in. Once you colour it in, you can tend to it, nurture it and amplify it. I would rather spend my time doing this instead of searching in all the wrong places feeling lost, frustrated and scattered.

Before doing the Process and gaining this awareness, your Soul Purpose picture may look like a massive mess of black dots all over the page. No order, no structure, no clear path.

How often do you wake up in the morning and just amble through life, feeling like you have no energy?

"X" Marks the Spot - Soul Purpose

Every past event in your life has been a dot on your Soul Purpose Masterpiece. When you join all the dots, you will gain laser focused clarity on your Soul Purpose and why you are here on this earth. Your dots are waiting to be joined!

Your masterpiece is waiting to be coloured, primped, primed with all the gold trimmings.

All my products and services are in some way designed with this in mind. It is lovingly designed to REMIND YOU OF YOUR POWER - which funnily enough is part of my Soul Purpose Masterpiece. To help you uncover and anchor in your SOUL PURPOSE.

To expose, find each dot, dust it off and make it part of the bigger picture. To remind you who you were before all the stuff happened to you. Before you became a parent, before the trauma, before the heartache, before the limiting beliefs and also to understand that those painful events are all little dots in a much bigger picture; with a much bigger purpose.

YOUR PURPOSE.

Each experience is on the way, not in the way. Each moment is a dot in your Soul Purpose Masterpiece.

Let's uncover your dots.

I have several heartfelt products which help uncover and intensify your connection to your purpose and power. They are there to help you illuminate the dots and go through the process of joining them so you can see your BIG PICTURE.

I created a Sterling Silver jewellery range called *Remember Ring Jewellery*. It includes the Ascension 2 Remember ring, Ascension 2 Charm necklace and Rise Up, Soul Sister earrings.

These magical pieces are so powerful; anchoring women all over the world to their purpose and power. I also create a deck of Pixie Affirmation Cards.

Each Pixie in the deck is a man or woman from Those 2 Sisters community who I admire and have inspired me in their journey. There are 37 cards in the deck and these beautiful community members messages get spread across the globe daily through this deck of Pixie Cards.

One of my most popular products is a subscription model, the online Monthly Mastermind. It has the SOUL PURPOSE PROCESS in it. The exact strategy I personally use, and all my students complete to uncover their Purpose Picture.

It is deep and intense - and it works. We break your life dots down and then take some time to join them all together. We also do a version of this process at my Soul Mastery Retreats every year. I currently run two retreats a year however I am looking at increasing it as it keeps selling out!

My Rise and Shine Podcasts Series touches on the topic of Soul Purpose regularly, as I use all the different layers, language and techniques to help even more people discover their Soul Purpose.

"X" Marks the Spot - Soul Purpose

One of the very first podcasts I did was called "Discover Your Soul Purpose." I interviewed my older sister, Michelle Anne. It was terrible, because it was only the third one I recorded, I didn't have a proper microphone, there was terrible background noise, and no intro or outro. It was so unprofessional. I think we might have even sung (terribly) at some point through the podcast. Hahaha.

However, the content itself is LIFE CHANGING so I have left it up and it is one of the podcasts I get the most feedback from. Hundreds of people contacted me to tell me they had their ah-ha moment through listening to this podcast.

Side note: Mumma's, don't wait for things to be perfect to launch them. Just take action and get it out. This comes easier when you are on Purpose (just another dot on the Masterpiece) as what people think of you is less relevant when your focus is on IMPACT and SERVICE.

When you own everything on the inside, nothing and no one can touch you on the outside.

My first Amazon Best Seller book is called "Rise up, The Soulful Guide to Success" and is available as an eBook, Hard Copy or Audio.

Because this process and topic has been the game changer in my life and business, I have also based my half-day workshop, *"6 Steps to Soul Success"* around it.

If you are interested in any of the above products or joining us on this journey to live your life on PURPOSE and complete my life- changing Purpose Process, you can visit my website www.dianemckendrick.com and order any products or book in for my events.

Using the above as an example, all those products on their own, don't mean much and as single products and services, they would get lost in the noise of the industry. Just a single dot. However, after doing my dot-to-dot picture, I realised that ALL of these products are dots on my Soul Purpose Masterpiece.

When grouped together, they paint a picture and tell a story. The nature and intention of them collectively reflect my Soul Purpose.

EDUCATE, INSPIRE AND EMPOWER.

REMIND WOMEN OF THEIR POWER, BY BEING IN MINE.

So, do you want to know how to pinpoint your Soul Purpose so you can wake up every day on purpose and live the life you were born for?

Let's get started with some questions for the beginning of your Soul Purpose Masterpiece:

From the ages of 1-10, what were your biggest voids?

e.g. Lack of attention from parents, money, intelligence etc.

"X" Marks the Spot - Soul Purpose

Your voids in childhood often become some of your biggest driving forces in adulthood. These dots often get missed in the picture, people discount them because it was so long ago.

___

From the ages of 11-21, what were your biggest voids?

e.g. Lack of attention from parents, money etc.

If you have felt a void of something all the way from birth through to the age of 21, you can be certain that it will govern some degree of your behaviour in adulthood.

___

What do you love to do?

___

TIME: *What do you spend the most time doing?*

___

Why do you do that?

___

SPACE: *What do you keep in your immediate space?*

___

Why is it important to you?

___

MONEY: *What do you spend the most money on?*

___

Why is that important to you?

___

COMMUNICATION: *What do you think about the most?*

___

ORGANISATION: *Where are you most ordered and organised?*

___

FOCUS: *Where are you most reliable, disciplined and focused?*

_____

SOCIAL: *What topics do you find yourself discussing in social settings most?*

_____

Before I sat with and got honest with the above answers, I was a mess. Pretending day after day and feeling lonely and disconnected. Internally, I was crumbling. My life, relationships, and finances all disjointed and disempowered.

The final question that put the cherry on top was truthfully answering all of the above and then asking:

"How can I do all of that while helping someone else?"

A great example of this is my older sister, Michelle Anne, Soul Healer. She is a police-officer-turned-spiritual-healer and now spends most of her days doing healing sessions and running retreats.

I remember just after I had gone through this process, we were sitting down over coffee discussing all things Soul Purpose. I asked her, *"What do you love to do?"*

She laughed, *"Chat to people and drink coffee! I can't really make a living or monetise drinking coffee and talking to people, though!"*

GUESS WHAT?

Several years later as we were taking our students through the 6 Steps to Soul Success at our half day workshop, she had an ah-ha moment.

She is now running a successful, heartfelt business. She used to work in a coffee shop for years as she was going through university and absolutely LOVED it. I worked there for about two months and absolutely HATED it – Haha!

Our different personalities shone through. She is far more of an extrovert than me.

It was the one dot she hadn't joined up in her Soul Purpose Masterpiece. Now one of her best-selling products is Cacao, a plant medicine which is drunk warm; an ancient ceremonial drink from the Andes. Connecting humans back to the earth, themselves and each other.

She also hosts a weekly Community Coffee for her clients. She doesn't charge for these events, she just loves to do it. Supporting others in community, connection and uncovering their purpose over a warm cup of cacao or coffee.

As these events were so popular and people wanted more, she launched monthly Cacao Circles. These events are very versatile, and she blends online and offline for our community.

"X" Marks the Spot - Soul Purpose

It was probably nearly 20 years ago when she made the remark about her Soul Purpose being *"Coffee, connection and talking to people."*

Her ego told her it was impossible. She put Missy in the back seat and went FULL steam ahead!

Asking yourself the above questions and finding yourself a like-minded community or group of people, will start to dig through the mountainous layers and get you to the core of WHY you are here on this earth.

It's time to create your Masterpiece that awaits you!

SUMMARY

- Your purpose is here and now, your closer to your purpose than what you think.

- SOUL PURPOSE is a specific calling from your soul.

- Your purpose is unique to you and it's not the same as anyone else.

- We are taught to look outside of ourselves for our Soul Purpose.

- It is PRESENT within you now, not something you move towards.

- All the events of your life which are like messy little dots on a piece of paper, once joined through my Purpose Process, will display a clear picture of your Soul Purpose Masterpiece.

- My products and services (which are part of my Soul Purpose Masterpiece) are designed to help you create yours and bring you HOME to your Soul Purpose Masterpiece.

- If you can truthfully answer the questions above and help others by doing what you love with people you love, your life will transform.

Chapter four

BRIDGE THE GAP TO A HIGHER STANDARD – VALUES

"It's not what you say. It's what you DO that will be the missing puzzle piece for many of you."
Diane McKendrick

This chapter will assist you in determining what is truly most important in YOUR life.

And we are going to drill down even deeper. Now that you are closer to your Soul Purpose, I am going to help you discover what is most inspiring in YOUR life. Let's find out what is most meaningful to YOU.

Once you have worked that out, life will be easier, and much more enjoyable! When you truly know what is important to you (your values), you can start to create a life in alignment with that, instead of constantly reacting to outside circumstances and pin balling from one pain or drama to the next.

For years I plodded along, not questioning anything at all. Following the status quo. Finished school, got a job, worked hard, saved money, got a promotion, got a better job - I literally chose the job from the job interview that gave me the first yes!

I showed up every morning, took lunch when they told me, took holidays when they told me! Worked more than I was paid for, I went out drinking with my friends on Friday, Saturday AND Sunday. I drank coffee with sugar and milk, because everyone else did (not noticing it caused bloating and pain) because bloating and pain was my normal. I started my morning with the news and newspapers because that is what I saw my parents do - I didn't question it. Monday would roll around and I would do it all over again!

I'm not saying anything is wrong with the above, I was doing what I thought I was supposed to without any deeper reflection or understanding of who I was and what was important to ME.

I was on autopilot. Like a robot just doing what was expected by society. Once I discovered what was most important to me, I started to make subtle changes, so I could experience more of the things that I enjoyed. Slowly but surely, I started to make sustainable and subtle changes, so I could invest my time and space with people, things and ideas that are important and valuable TO ME!

Most people live a life trying to fill a void as they are trying to live up to a subconscious standard; expectations of a parent, teacher, preacher or friend. We often subconsciously try to create a life around what is important to THEM.

There are a number of reasons we do this:

1. To fit in.
2. To please and appease our nearest and dearest.
3. To make our parents proud.
4. To be accepted.
5. To be the good girl.
6. To not rock the boat.
7. Because we don't know any other way.

We confuse what is really important to us individually to what we think it should be, ought to be or could be; which is determined by what we are told and demonstrated by others as we grow up.

The worst thing is most of us don't even realise we are doing it! Like me for the first 30 years of my life.

Here is a clue: You may be reacting to your life or living other peoples, society or cultural beliefs and values.

Observe your internal dialogue. If you notice these words or phrases in your language, then this may be the case:

I should do.
I ought to do.
I need to do.
I got to do.
I must do.
I have to do.

You feel as though you have a duty to do the thing, instead of simply doing what you really LOVE and feeling called and inspired to do. When you feel like you *have* to do something, it becomes a chore and it disempowers you, exhausts you and will move you further away from your truth.

How many of us feel the constant pang of what we *should* be doing?

Tony Robbins calls it, *"Shoulding all over yourself!"*

Hahahaha.

Are you shoulding all over yourself?

Take some time now to notice where you use these words and how they make you feel.

Bridge The Gap To A Higher Standard – Values

To counteract the above, when I observe myself or my clients using the above dialogue, I simply ask, *"Says who? Who says I should/need/have/ must do something?"*

99% of the time its someone close to you; often your parents or main caregivers as you were growing up.

Many of us, myself included, prior to doing this work, created a life, relationship, job, around what we are told by our adult role models around us as we grow up. From birth, we learn to pattern their behaviours and their emotional states. We learn what is important to them and then go about our lives matching that.

We rarely stop and ask, *"What is true for me?"* as we naturally take what our caregivers and elders say as gospel and go about like busy little bees trying to create a fulfilled life for ourselves while doing things that please others and are important to them - and not ourselves.

As a society, we are NOT encouraged to be leaders and stand out.

From a young age, we are taught to *"Do what we are told."*

When you stand out, there is risk of ridicule and humiliation so many of us take the easy option and subconsciously follow the unspoken rules and regulations of our culture, society and family traditions.

As a result, there are so many of us in the 2000's who feel lost, isolated, depleted, depressed and lonely. Unknowingly, we hear and action the voices in our head of our parents, teachers, preachers, caregivers and give that more attention than the whisper of OUR soul. That soft gentle voice reminding you were destined for more, that soft sweet voice that reminds you:

You are different. You are special. You are born for greatness.

After I help my clients work through the above and start making empowered choices for their life, a "higher level challenge" presents itself.

What do I mean by a higher-level challenge?

Let me explain.

This was a game changer for me in my Motherhood, Money, Mindset and all other areas of my life.

I noticed myself constantly trying to "put out fires" before they even started. Every time I was presented with a challenge, I felt like it was because I had made a mistake, or it was fundamentally my fault that the thing happened. I constantly felt like I failed because I believed if I had done something differently; been more organised, took more time, planned better than I could have avoided the mistake.

I now call this a 'challenge' instead of a mistake. Even by changing the word mistake to challenge, makes a huge difference.

A challenge is an adventure that I get to learn from and overcome, I welcome them and embrace them.

Bridge The Gap To A Higher Standard – Values

A mistake is something that's gone wrong because of what I did or didn't do, it makes me feel flawed and like nothing I do is right and feels like a dark cloud that follows me around, making my life hard.

Once again, a simple change of language goes a long way.

I learnt that life is literally a string of challenges and as we evolve and up-level our way of life and thinking the challenges we experience along the way also become a higher-level problem or challenge.

For example, my first challenge was that I was 20kg overweight. So, I decided to join a gym. My next challenge was working out how I was going to pay for the gym. Instead of just feeling guilty about spending money, I knew that it was a better problem to have then just feel fat, overweight, and uncomfortable in my clothes.

After I found a way to pay for the gym, the next challenge was finding a babysitter for my kids while I worked out. Again, if I got lost in the problem and started blaming myself, I wouldn't have taken any action.

I reminded myself, this is STILL a better problem to have, than feeling fat, overweight, and having physical and mental health issues. All I need to do was find a babysitter while I worked out.

So, now I've found a way to work out, pay for it, get my kids looked after and my next problem was, I'm so sore I can barely walk. Now I need some supplements to support my growth and healing in the gym. My challenge - I couldn't afford them, but I reminded myself that finding money to buy protein powder is once again a better problem to have then having to go to the doctor and find money to pay for tests to tell me why I'm so lethargic and tired. Now I have more energy, I'm moving, I'm in an environment where the majority of people are focused on health and how they do life is different.

NB: I just launched my own Protein Blend, customised for women on this journey with me, so the next high-level challenge was getting the confidence to talk to Nutritionist and Food Technicians. Notice how our life levels up, as do our challenges. As we raise the standard of our life, we raise the standard of our challenges.

If I look at each challenge on its own, not in context of the whole picture, it's easy to get caught up in the "mistake jungle." To judge myself, give myself a hard time and blame myself for the mistakes with the knock-on effect is usually procrastination, stagnation and self-loathing. None of which is very productive in building a million-dollar business or parenting two young kids! Or anything else for that matter.

Remember, whatever challenges you are experiencing in your life, not to get caught in the mistake jungle.

Understand, life is a series of challenges and as you evolve and level up, so do your challenges. Take a moment to think about high level challenges now.

So, what is the high-level challenge that pops up for many of my clients when evolving very rapidly by connecting back to their true purpose, uncovering their core values and what is important to THEM, whilst dissolving fear, guilt or paradox's keeping them stuck and digging deep?

Who wants to guess what it is? The next high-level challenge is actually realising:

YOU ARE MORE FEARFUL OF THE GREATNESS OF YOUR LIGHT THAN THE SADNESS OF YOUR DARK!

There is a small percentage of you (similar to me) who won't follow the status quo and will question what we have been taught and will commit to your GREATNESS; who will shine their light. Step up and out of the mistake jungle and seek higher level challenges.

We will be the voice, we will be the change and we will guide others to stand up and make their own decisions instead of reacting to the unfolding world around them.

Which one are you?

Do you know what your values are? Or are you prepared to explore deeper and get to know yourself better, to trust your YOURSELF and your deepest desires and create a life to reflect that? Or are you playing it safe and caught in the game of "fitting in," running around getting caught in the quick sand of the mistake jungle? Wasting time in paradox and procrastination as you try to please and appease others but feel dead on the inside, pin balling between jobs, relationships, health challenges, struggling to pay the bills?

By taking the time to determine YOUR values and bringing them to the surface, we can commit to designing and creating your life around them.

This is probably singularly one of the most powerful insights I have had on my self-development journey. Once you pinpoint your values, you will experience a deep sense of self. Inner peace, possibility, abundance and a childlike curiosity and excitement will become your default states and emotions.

You will feel wholesome and excited about life and what you can contribute.

You will embrace your high-level challenges.

Excited every night to go to bed because you get to wake up the next day and do what you love, with people you love and excited every morning to wake up because of what you can contribute, create and share with the world. You get endless amounts of energy and things just seem to work.

Life is easy and enjoyable from here.

This is where you will be your most creative and innovative, in your area of genius.

This is where you will get your energy, drive, motivation from.

Too many of you are still looking in the *Weetbix* box or *Milo* tin for your motivation. Seeking it externally.

I'm telling you, it's not there! It's within you NOW.

Bridge The Gap To A Higher Standard – Values

We just have to take some time to join all the dots!

To uncover what is truly important to YOU at the core.

Once this concept pops for you, your heart and head will be in coherence, working together rather than against each other.

Nobody is exempt from this.

Everybody has a set of values in life, a set of priorities and whatever is highest on that values list, whatever is really truly most important to you is also known as "your purpose."

Most people are too busy "looking for it" or "working for it" to see that we have it literally at our fingertips.

Often when I ask my clients about values, they will say things like honestly, integrity, and peace. These are not our values, they are ideals.

To determine your values, look at what your life DEMONSTRATES. Not what you say. What you say has been taught to you. It is coming from the filter of parents, caregivers, culture and society.

Look at what your life currently demonstrates.

You will find time, space and resources for the things you value.

If you say you value your family but spend 15 hours a day at work, your actions are demonstrating, your highest value is NOT your family. You might want or think it should be your family.

However, your life is demonstrating your truth.

If your highest value was family, you would find a way to spend time and space with them while creating an income. Many of you might say, *"But Di, I'm at work to get money to support my family."*

In which case, your higher value is money or the other things that work is giving you. If family was your number one value, you would find a way to support them and create income for them while spending time and space with them.

Always look at what your life demonstrates, not what you "think" is the answer.

My life changed by reading books like this and doing exercises like the ones I've included in this book. Watch your WHOLE LIFE transform.

So, you might be pondering the questions, what are my values? And how do I find them?

To find your current values, we are going to dissect your current life and pinpoint what your past and current actions, behaviours, environments and thoughts demonstrate.

Again, not what you say. It's what you DO that will be the missing puzzle piece for many of you! We will look at what you currently spend your time, effort, energy on and what you keep in close proximity in your environment.

Bridge The Gap To A Higher Standard – Values

I have a questionnaire I personally use and with all of my clients, which you can access from *www.dianemckendrick.com/values*

In this book, I have included the first several questions and if you want the rest, please pop over to the website to download the complete list with the explanation video.

It is important that you answer these questions with what is true for you RIGHT NOW; what is currently being demonstrated in your life.

Not what you "think" or "say" or what you want in the future. Actually, what it is NOW.

The answers are often so easy and close to you, you miss them.

You are subconsciously competent which is why so many people miss the cues. Remember again, through this process, it is important that you look at what is currently demonstrated in your life and answer with what actually IS.

QUESTIONS

1. What do you fill your space with?
2. What do you fill your time with?
3. What energises you?
4. What do you spend money on?
5. Where are you organised?
6. Where are you most disciplined and reliable?

For the explanation video and your complete copy of the questionnaire, visit www.dianemckendrick.com/values/

These questions seem simple and easy and prior to completing them for myself the first time, I found myself asking, *"How are these piddly little questions going to change my life?"*

Well, they did.

Once I got clear on the above, I was able to redesign my entire life. I lost weight and got fit and healthy again. I no longer got sick every few weeks. I got out of a full-time role in the corporate world which was sucking my soul dry and created my own Personal Training business. I started spending time with people who supported and encouraged me instead of gossiped or criticized me. I still didn't have much money, but I realised that was because it was at the bottom of my values list. At least I knew now so I could make the appropriate changes.

Through this questionnaire and my research on values, I realised that health was my highest priority which meant that I created routines that supported that. It was also shown to me that relationships were high on the list, as was spirituality. As demonstrated in my life, money was one of the least important to me.

In my new model of the world that I chose, I wanted more money. I wanted it to be important, so I could create financial freedom. I was saying it was important, but my behaviour, space and environment was not suggesting that was true.

When I did the questions above, it helped me see that in fact I DID NOT VALUE money, even though the words I was saying said otherwise. What I was finally able to do was consciously choose!

I decided I wanted more money but not at the expense of my health or my relationships. So, I linked my lowest value of "money" to my highest value of "health." I did a linking process where I convinced my brain that I could improve my health if I could afford organic food, if I could buy the best supplements and see the best natural health professionals.

The moment I linked money with being able to improve my health, my money blueprint shifted, and I instantly started to get more of it. Because of the change in my mindset, I spent my time researching wealth creation and started taking actions to increase and improve my net worth.

Now, because of the questions above and the information in this book, I am on track to become a millionaire within the next two years, while building a business that supports and encourages ALL of my main values; health, connection, relationships, wealth, financial freedom and contribution.

I could not have done this unless I started at the very beginning and got rid of all the injected beliefs, values and ideas injected by external sources.

There are things in life that YOU love, that are important to YOU.

So, what are you waiting for?

Millionaire Mum

Get cracking on the exercise above and uncover what your core values are so you can create the life, relationships, body and business of YOUR DREAMS!

Welcome in your higher-level challenges.

As your life evolves so do your challenges.

Embrace them and use them to your advantage.

Bridge The Gap To A Higher Standard – Values

SUMMARY:

- When you truly know what is important to you (your values), you can start to create a life in alignment with that, instead of constantly reacting to outside circumstances and pin balling from one pain or drama to the next.

- Most of us are living someone else's values which have been subconsciously injected into us from birth by caregivers, society and culture.

- Most of us don't question things, we just do what we know and what we were taught.

- Your language can be a clue if you are living your truth or someone else's.

- We are NOT encouraged to be leaders and stand out.

- Instead of listening to the whispers of your soul, most people are inundated and listening to the voices in their head. Which is the voice of our caregivers.

- As we do this work we evolve as do our challenges. We get higher-level problems which keep us out of the mistake jungle.

- Most people are more afraid of their greatness, their light then their dark.

- Only a small percentage of you will do the work.

- Most people are too busy "looking for it" or "working for it" to see it in that we have it at our fingertips.

- To determine your values, look at what your LIFE DEMONSTRATES. Not what you say.

- Once you pinpoint your values you will experience a deep sense of self. Inner peace, possibility, abundance and a childlike curiosity and excitement will become your default states and emotions

- You can change your values once you become aware of them. You can link your lower values with your higher ones.

Chapter five

FROZEN: CONQUERING FEAR

*"Fear is a function of the mind, it keeps you safe.
Pinpoint your Fear and set yourself FREE."
Diane McKendrick*

By now, you should have a deeper understanding of and committed to:

- Choosing a starting point.
- Connecting with who you REALLY ARE (without all the stuff).
- Discovering, feeling and living your "WHY" and understanding your role here on this earth.
- Your wheel is plumping out and you acknowledge that regardless how hard, uncomfortable and awkward it is - it's all part of the journey.
- You know now that "self-esteem" is only part of the process and that "fluffy affirmations don't work."
- You have uncovered your VALUES and are designing a life in alignment with your CORE VALUES.

Know all this now, my next question for you is:

What will stop you from living this LIFE of love and freedom, passion and purpose?

Who/where/what will freeze you in your tracks, keep you looping at the bottom of the pit, have you second-guessing yourself, creating arguments, dramas and self-sabotaging patterns?

I'll tell ya what, I'll tell ya who, I'll tell ya where... FEAR. That's what!

The only reason you won't go and act on these things is fear. You have fears that haven't been dissolved yet.

This chapter will help you understand fear and give you a different relationship with your mind. My intention is to deepen your awareness and give you a very specific process to rewire the mind and eliminate/dissolve fear, so you can do, be and have whatever you want in this lifetime.

Once you comprehend and embody this process, you learn how to pinpoint the fear, dissolve it. There will be nothing and no one that can stop you.

YOU WILL TAKE INSPIRED ACTION WITH FOCUSED INTENTION.

This is when your whole life will really transform.

If you have found your truth and it,'s soul-guided, purpose/value based, you will become unstoppable in all areas of your life.

This is my mission and my personal dream to give you a wholesome approach to life.

Not just one area but ALL areas equally. Physique, business, finances, relationships, ALL areas of your life.

Here are a few guiding questions to ask yourself in my personal process of DISSOLVING this concept we call FEAR:

1. What actually is fear?
2. What does it feel like?
3. Where do you feel it in your body?
4. When did you last feel it?
5. What does it look like?

When I learnt what I am about to share here, my whole life was TRANSFORMED.

Cognitively, I still felt it stuck in my body. I was embodying FEAR. Debilitated, crippled and stuck on the hamster wheel stressed, overwhelmed, overweight, procrastinating, making excuses and barely getting by. Fear was running and ruining my life, even though I knew cognitively that it wasn't real.

It had never been explained to me the way I am about to share it with you now. When I finally put all the content, experiences, and information together, I created this theory for myself, my family and my clients. And now I get to share it with you.

By learning what fear is and how it is created in our mind, changed my relationship to it – BEFORE I even approached the Dissolve Fear process.

The first thing to explore is the idea of the past, present and future.

In the mind, the future represents imagination and the past represents memory. Therefore, the first thing to understand is that the future and past doesn't really exist beyond the realm of the mind. If you're having a hard time gripping this, answer these questions:

1. What is the future?
2. Where is the future?
3. Can you go to it?

You can only THINK about the future and THINK about the past. You can't go to the future because when you get to the future, it will be a new PRESENT moment. You will be in a new PRESENT MOMENT with its own future and past.

For example, at some point in the future, let's just say next year, you will be there at that point in time, and it will simply be a new PRESENT moment with its own future and past.

You can only access the PAST in memory and you can only access the FUTURE in imagination.

Therefore, these concepts of Future and Past are only a function of the mind. They don't really exist outside the realm of our mind in terms of memory and imagination.

All that FEAR is, is a FUTURE IMAGINATION of something NEGATIVE happening to YOU.

Something that has more negative than positive, something that is mainly negative that you are imagining in the future coming TOWARDS YOU. Imagining that the negative thing is going to happen to you.

COMMON FEARS

- Fear of failing
- Fear of being betrayed
- Fear of losing money
- Fear of being humiliated and outcast

- Fear of being rejected
- Fear of losing life

ADD YOURS HERE

_____

_____

_____

_____

_____

Fear is an imagination and an assumption that at some point in the future, you're going to experience more pain than pleasure, more negative than positive, more drawbacks than benefits, more challenges than support.

The next concept to grasp is that:

YOU CAN'T HAVE AN IMAGINATION WITHOUT A MEMORY.

Imagination is a mirror of your memory.

Read that again:

YOU CAN'T HAVE AN IMAGINATION WITHOUT A MEMORY!

IMAGINATION is a MIRROR of your MEMORY.

Every future imagination with perceived negative without positive coming toward you (FEAR) will be mirrored in the past by a memory of a perceived negative without a positive coming towards YOU. It will be a mirror image in the mind.

To clear your fear, we need to rewind the memory bank to the specific moment in time in the past (a memory), where you perceived more negative charge than positive, more drawback than benefit which your brain has "logged" as a negative or scary event.

For example, if you were cheated on in a relationship you may have a fear of relationships in the future as there is a charge in your memory of a painful relationship.

Remember your FUTURE mirrors your PAST.

Likewise, you might have been ripped off or humiliated in the past and have the "negatively charged memory" logged, therefore you almost certainly will be FEARFUL of getting ripped off in the future.

Another popular fear is "fear of failing." It's simply because you have a logged memory of the perception of failing and have only attached to one side of the coin. Only remembering the NEGATIVE. Once again, your future will mirror your past!

As with nature, in actuality to be WHOLE, everything has both NEGATIVE and POSITIVE charge. This includes your memories and your imaginations. This is science.

When we attach to one or the other, our life is out of balance. We feel in limbo and like a cannon ball swinging pendulum with no direction or focus. We become disillusioned, depressed, scared living in flight or fright. Or we swing to the other side of the pendulum bringing in ALL the positive and living in fantasy or infatuation which is as equally debilitating.

The place of power is TRUTH and PRESENCE which is when you are centred and poised. Not caught or attached to either end of the spectrum.

I often witness people in fantasy or infatuation in their relationship. They think when they get the "perfect person," their life will be PERFECT. Other examples include, *"When I get the job promotion, I'll be happy. Everything will be perfect then."*

Once again, be reminded of the same concept.

Nothing is ever ALL positive or ALL negative.

We need to remember that there is an equal and opposite to every positive and every negative and when you understand and embody these concepts and theories I'm sharing, life gets easier. We enter into what I call flow state; operating from Truth and Presence and it's like you have the Keys of the Kingdom.

In order to dissolve these fears and fantasies, I have a process I take you through in my Online Mastermind which walks you through step by step, using the functionality of your brain to neutralise each remembered charge or memory. The full explanation with diagrams and spreadsheets to log your memories, emotions and charges are included in my Online Mastermind.

The magic happens with the synthesis of the positive and negative charge.

My Online Mastermind is delicately set out to guide you through your personal Fear Dissolving Process. Each Masterclass Class and Module give you specific detailed videos with diagrams, spreadsheets, formulas of what I explained through this chapter (and book).

I guide you through the specific questioning that you need to ask in order to find out what is the fear for you, what's the associated charges from the past (memory) which are stored and sorted in your mind as a resentment; something negative which happened to you in the past and you not seeing the other side of it. Through the process, I show you how to bring those charges to the surface and through the synthesis of positive and negative.

We dissolve the fear through the dialogue and questioning process. We set you free.

Having done this process hundreds of times now and freed thousands of people globally from their debilitating fears, I notice a few common obstacles. I have many clients who know they are scared of "something" because it shows up in their life, however when I question them further, it's like their brain blocks them from answering. They chunk their answers up to something like, *"I'm scared of failing,"* or *"I'm scared looking like a loser in front of my friends and family,"* or *"I'm scared of being cheated on."*

When we dig deeper because their brain perceives the memory as "painful," it stops them from accessing it easily. It's also a new pattern you will be running in your brain; as with everything it takes time and practise.

The first time I did the Process, it took me an hour. Now, I can literally do it in a few moments.

Until you can access the precise moment of charge, or the memory, we can't fully dissolve the fear. So, what we can do is reverse engineer from the imagination. Often, it's a memory from childhood when you were ashamed and embarrassed for getting something wrong, being made to look like a loser in front of your family and friends.

YOUR FEARS ARE NOT RANDOM. There will be an EXACT MOMENT of charge in your memory of an event that relates to the fear.

The first few times I took myself through this process I cleared the big things like:

- Fear of not being good enough
- Fear of failing and looking like a loser
- Fear of being bullied by my peers of colleagues
- Fear of losing money or getting into debt
- Fear of being found out as a fraud

I slowly worked my way through these and each one I cleared gave me more freedom and space to be me. To share my voice with the world, to step up and be seen and heard. To create a conscious, compassionate community and step into my role as a Compassionate Leader.

Let's look at where a few of these fears came from for me in the past.

When I started my authoring journey to write my first book: I was crippled with chronic, debilitating fear. This fear physically affected my body to the point where I could barely move. Interestingly, this injury happened the weekend of my Author's Retreat in Melbourne.

I didn't know the Fear Process at the time but have since worked my way through it to clear the fear of not being good enough. The memory that gave rise to the fear was right back from when I was 15 years old.

I was a National Level athlete gifted with physical attributes and the mindset to compliment it. Because of this talent and lifestyle, I created a belief that I was a "dummy" in the classroom. My sister, in comparison, was a super smartie (and she used to get teased for being so smart). To my 15-year-old brain, her academic ability meant that I was even more dumb and not good enough.

NOTE: This is all subconscious. At the time, I had NO IDEA I thought like this, I just knew that as an adult, I felt like a dummy and never good enough, like I was fundamentally flawed and everything I did I either majorly stuffed up or quit.

This charge and process was uncovered through the Fear Process.

At first, I couldn't find the memory, it's kind of a weird thing to do. It felt awkward and uncomfortable and I had spent years saying fluffy positive affirmations to fill this void. Pretending it wasn't there. So, to actually face it head on was confronting. Something I had been hiding from myself and the world since I could remember.

As I went back through my memory bank, a few memories came flooding back to me.

The first one was in Grade 2. The class was learning to count in 2's. I was seven years old. I tried so hard, but my mind would NOT grasp the concept of 2,4,6,8,10 so I was the last kid in the class to "get it." Our teacher would make us stand up in front of everyone and count in 2's, every single morning.

Day after day for several days, I was horrified, embarrassed, ashamed, dreading going to school because I felt so useless. I was ridiculed in front of the whole class, with each time ending with everyone laughing at me as I fumbled my way through and got it wrong, every damn time.

By the last day, I remember the teacher being frustrated with me as I could still not grasp the concept. I was petrified. Every time she put me on the spot, my brain would go blank. She made me stand on the chair in front of the whole class and reprimanded me.

Frozen: Conquering FEAR

I was literally the last kid standing.

I ended up in tears, and still didn't learn to count in 2's. The memory created a limiting belief and fears of:

"I'm not good enough."
"No one likes me."
"I'm a dummy."
"I'm scared to stand in front of people in case I freeze and they laugh at me."
"I'm scared of numbers, I don't understand them."
"I'm scared to try new things in case I stuff it up."

The next memory that popped up was also at school. Grade 10 this time, 15-years-old.

By now, my swimming career was in full swing. I was deadly shy, timid and could barely say a word to anyone. Even my swimming coach. I decided to jump in the deep end and choose Speech and Drama as an elective for my subjects as when I watched those girls speak and perform on stage, it moved me. The impact, power, poise, grace and beauty they displayed was mystical to me. So, I signed up because I was terrible at it and I wanted to get better.

The school called my parents and said, *"There must be some mistake. Diane's signed up for Speech and Drama."*

My mum came to me and asked me, and I shyly said I wanted to do it to learn how to speak and share the stage like the other girls I had seen.

Millionaire Mum

The school didn't let me do Speech and Drama as an elective subject because I was so extremely terrible at it.

To top this memory off, my last presentation of the year before we went into the senior year. I memorised my whole seven-minute presentation. I wanted to show them that I COULD do it. I was so focused on memorising and reciting my speech that I literally forgot to breathe for the whole seven minutes.

By the time I finished, my face was bright red. I was sweating profusely, and I looked like a deer in headlights. I looked at my teacher for moral support and a smirk pulled at the creases of her mouth. She tried hard not to laugh but it came... BIG. She bellowed out with laughter across the whole classroom which gave subconscious permission for everyone else in the classroom to laugh at me.

I was mortified.

It was one of those moments you wish the floor would open up and swallow you!

Through her laughter she sputtered out, *"That was the funniest thing I've ever seen."*

This memory created the belief and fears:

"No matter how hard I try, I'll fail."
"Fear of being outcast, rejected and ridiculed."
"I'm scared to speak in front of people."
"I felt betrayed by the teacher so felt scared to trust people."

Frozen: Conquering FEAR

DREAMS of inspiring, moving and impacting from the stage... GONE.

All my prior fears and self-loathing beliefs resurfaced. Knowing what I know now, these events were starting to form clusters in my memory bank. Reminder: your future or imagination is a mirror to your memory. In each of these memories, my subconscious has only pulled in the perceived negative charge.

In my adult years, all my prior fears and self-loathing beliefs resurfaced, renewed and replayed with a vengeance.

Reminder: Your future or imagination is a mirror to your memory of the past.

In the precise moments of charge, in each of these memories I only pulled in the negative. And so, I kept recreating it.

I kept the fear alive.

I was scared of these things happening to me AGAIN IN THE FUTURE and I didn't even know it. Being the creative, little being I am, I kept recreating it with great conviction over and over and over again in my life.

These fears filtered through to my body, my physique, my relationships, my finances and of course, memories in these areas where duplicates of the internal representation of the fundamental fears I remembered, and therefore projected forward.

I know this is a bit of a mind bend but stay with me.

Fast forward 30 years, with all the personal development, spiritual exploration and connection to the creator and my higher self. The messages came through from the Angels that I needed to write a book and share myself from stage. Every cell of my being screamed in horror and fear, *"NOOOOOOOO!"*

THE FEAR stopped me in my tracks.

It wasn't until I fully understood the concepts and theories I'm sharing in this book that my life, business, body, relationships and finances really took a quantum leap!

Are you ready to take a quantum leap with me?

My higher self; smiles sweetly with a knowing and resounding, *"YEEEESSSSS!"*

After I moved through a few of these big challenges and fears, my life and business started to skyrocket. I realised soon into the journey that there was an underlying fear still present and I played around in the vortex for a while to discover what it was.

Soon, my dreams were coming true before my eyes.

My first book got published and won Best Seller. My first Four Weeks to Freedom Online Mastermind sold out. My merchandise was getting shipped all over the world. My Sterling Silver jewellery range helping to anchor women globally to their power. My clothing line getting well received by our followers, as well as my 2nd Edition Pixie affirmation cards launched and SOLD OUT within minutes. My Soul Mastery Retreats fully booked out and getting booked and paid for exclusive speaking events. Completing my first three National Speaking tours. And my podcast getting published and hitting 2k subscribers.

I was shocked to find out that I had a FEAR OF SUCCESS. A fear that SUCCESS would have me exposed as a fraud; an imposter.

The moment I realised it, I cleared my whole afternoon of appointments and I logged on to my own online Mastermind as a client.

I listened to myself deliver, took notes, did my Fear Processes, worked my way through the modules and VOILA.

In less than an hour, I was FREE again.

It took me back to a memory of winning a GOLD medal at National School Girl Swimming titles. Which meant I was the fastest swimmer for my age in Australia. When I returned home with the gold medal, once again expecting praise and acceptance, I was met with my friendship group (one girl in particular) bullying and rejecting me. It lasted for weeks.

Once again, the memory of success being logged and stored with more negative than positive.

I also discovered I had guilt around WINNING.

The time that I swam to WIN was not my best time and was slower than usual for that age group. So, I felt like a fraud and I didn't deserve to win with that time, which of course, was where the fear of FRAUD was birthed.

Moving through the questioning process neutralised it for me and I went on my merry way.

Success is now part of my being.

It's wholesome, easy and fun. It's a way of life.

You may have noticed I have left the best until last and you are probably frothing to get the Guiding Questions to start to dissolve and neutralise your fears. It's a little more in depth than just typing out a few questions.

I will add the main ones here to get you started but be sure to either pop over to my Online Mastermind and get your free 7-day trial.

GUIDING QUESTIONS

What is the specific fear?

_____

What is the memory?

_____

Frozen: Conquering FEAR

What was the benefit of that event happening?

_____

At the precise moment of charge, what was the opposite to what you perceived as the negative? e.g. What would have been the best-case scenario (the fantasy or infatuation) and list the drawback of the best-case scenario happening?

_____

_____

_____

_____

If the fear comes true, what are the benefits to you?

_____

_____

SUMMARY:

- The only thing stopping you is FEAR.

- COMMON FEARS

    Fear of failing

    Fear of being betrayed

    Fear of losing money

    Fear of being humiliated and outcast

    Fear of being rejected

    Fear of losing life

- Once you understand and dissolve fear you will take massive inspired action with focused intention

- If you have found your truth and its soul guided, purpose/value based you will become unstoppable in all areas of your life after you dissolve fear

- Future and Past are simply functions of the mind. They do not exist apart from in your memory or in your imagination. When you get to a time point in the future. e.g. next week, next year. It is simply a new PRESENT moment with its own future and past.

- You can't have an imagination without a memory

- Fear is simply a perceived painful memory of the past being projected or mirrored into the future.

- Dissolve the perceived negative charge logged in your subconscious mind through the guiding questions process to clear the fear.

- The place of power is TRUTH and PRESENCE. From this place we enter into a flow state, operating from Truth and Presence and it's like you have the Keys of the Kingdom.

- Fantasy and Infatuation are the opposite to fear and has the same effect.

- Until you can access the precise moment of charge (the memory) we can't fully dissolve the fear. Sometimes we need to reverse engineer.

Chapter Six

WRONG WAY: GO BACK AND DROP THE B/S"

"Don't believe your brain, it tells you what it thinks."
Diane McKendrick

This book was birthed from a limiting belief.

Prior to writing this book, I believed I couldn't be a good Mum AND a Millionaire. I had separated them in my mind and my belief was that I could either be a bad-ass business woman, kick butt and make waves in the industry OR a present, nurturing, stay-at-home Mum.

They were mutually exclusive, and I couldn't be, do and have both. I could have one or the other. I had to choose, and it meant I would have to sacrifice the other one.

Not a surprise, considering that was my belief. To be honest, I wasn't doing either very well.

I was internally torn, and I struggled daily to make ends meet. I constantly felt guilty, ashamed and almost ALWAYS resented either my business or my kids (or my husband) because I was so exhausted and miserable... So, that had to be his fault right!?

I didn't even realise until recently, but I had a deep-seeded belief that women were not meant to make money.

I believed millionaires were men.

This belief was uncovered when I read a book and it said, *"Visualise a millionaire."* I played along with the game, closed my eyes and up pops this image of a man in a suit carrying a suitcase.

Mmmm... I was further away than I thought. If you want more money in your life, I invite you to do the same. Shut your eyes, visualise a millionaire.

What do you see?

Wrong Way: Go Back And Drop The B/S"

Hopefully you see YOUR face smiling back at you. I do now.

I also believed in order to be wealthy, it meant that I was greedy. When I was 12-years-old, I heard a rich man say, *"If you want to be rich, you have to be willing to take food from the table of another family."*

I subconsciously decided at that moment, I would NEVER be rich. Why? Because I believed it meant others had to starve or sacrifice if I was wealthy.

Goooooodneesss meeeeeeeeee! Are any of these stories sounding familiar?

How many of you out there are staying stuck or hiding because of beliefs we have picked up along the way that we don't even know about?!

I'm a self-confessed, self-development junkie and still these beliefs were flying under the radar. So, go deep, don't let any of them go unattended or they will create havoc in your life.

To add a cherry on the top, I believed that, *"People didn't like rich women because almost every single one I've seen in the movies have been displayed as a massive, hard-ass bitch."*

The total opposite to the wise, gentle nurturing Mumma that I am. I couldn't possibly be both while I was believing all that baloney.

But wait… There's more.

Millionaire Mum

I believed that in order to earn money, I would have to work hard and long hours away from my kids. Funnily enough, back when that was my belief, I was working long hard hours away from my kids but still wasn't making much money.

Probably because I wasn't a man, right?!

WRONG.

It was because I believed all that rubbish! That's exactly what it all was! Rubbish! And you have some rubbish, too. It's time to take the rubbish out and start anew.

At the risk of simplifying it, you are what you think.

So, choose your thoughts wisely.

Even in the few seconds it's taken to read this sentence, you would have had several thoughts passing through your mind.

Take a moment to notice them. Yes YOU, reading this book. You had a thought just then. Write it down here:

_____

_____

Whatever we think about ourselves becomes the truth for us.

Every thought we think is creating our future.

Wrong Way: Go Back And Drop The B/S"

Let's play a little game. I can hear you thinking, *"Oh no, not another game!"* or maybe, *"Ooooh, what kinda game?"*

See! Another thought!

Write down (with no filter) what you thought when I said, *"Let's play a little game."*

_____

_____

Now take a photo and Facebook message it to me on my personal Facebook page - Diane McKendrick!

I want to see how many of you are ready to change.

Let me guess - you're having another thought, *"Photo? What? I didn't sign up for this. I want quiet reading time, I'm not taking a photo!"* or *"What's she talking about? I don't know how to use this thing to take a photo, let alone send it to her on Facebooky thing?!"* or even, *"She wants me to send her a photo! Ooohhh, I wonder if she will reply personally! Shit, she's gonna read it, I better make my answers GOOD!"*

Okay, woah. Hold your horses! Let's just breathe and try not to spiral...

So, tell me, what did you think?

Hahahaha! Now, send that to me!

Millionaire Mum

3,2,1 GO!

_____

_____

Okay, so now you are warmed up and ready for the game to start, I am going to say a word and I want you to write the first thoughts that comes into your mind.

Body:

_____

_____

Finances:

_____

_____

Relationships:

_____

_____

Wrong Way: Go Back And Drop The B/S"

Career:

_____

_____

Spirituality:

_____

_____

Love:

_____

_____

Life:

_____

_____

Now read back your answers and write below, how do they make you feel?

_____

_____

You might be feeling heavy, sad, overwhelmed, frustrated or perhaps you feel joyful and excited?

Circle the answer below. Would you like these thoughts to create your future? Do you want more of this for your life?

YES / NO

Thanks for playing!

Everything you think will eventually project itself outwards so it's important to monitor your internal thoughts and assess them regularly.

What you think determines how you feel and how you feel determines how you act.

So, if what you think ultimately determines, feelings and therefore actions, you may be asking where does the thought come from?

The thought comes from your internal belief systems or set of rules you have subconsciously created through life.

Wrong Way: Go Back And Drop The B/S"

We create our belief systems about ourselves and the world around us by the adults and relationships around us. It is most prevalent in the first eight years of our lives.

We model our relationships with others based on our relationship with Mum or Dad or in some cases, the relationship between Mum and Dad. We create our beliefs about our own self-worth by watching and learning from our parents on how they interact, nurture or scold themselves.

Have you noticed in life you often attract people that remind you of your parents? Either in a partner, friend or maybe even a boss at work?

There are predominately 2 types of beliefs:

1. EMPOWERING
2. LIMITING

I am going to give you my personal examples of the questions above and possible beliefs the answer originated from.

Take a look at my answers before I learnt what I am teaching your now about beliefs:

MISERABLE MUM ANSWERS
Body: Sore, heavy, tired, exhausted
Finances: Never enough, work hard, time away from family
Relationships: Hard work, painful
Career: Soul destroying, distraction, non-existent, fraud
Spirituality: What?

Love: I would but I'm too tired
Life: Boring and hard, torn

Doesn't take a rocket scientist to work out that the beliefs they were originating from and I was operating from where "limiting."

Here are the deep subconscious beliefs Miserable Diane held about these topics before I changed them:

BELIEFS OF MISERABLE MUM
Body: I'm not worth it.
Finances: There is never enough, my wealth means others misfortune.
Relationships: People are out to get me, I can't trust anyone.
Career: Work to get money, time away from family.
Spirituality: Religion is for lost people.
Love: I'm not worthy. It's hard to find.
Life: I don't deserve it.

In comparsion look at the answers from Diane, Millionaire Mum

MILLIONAIRE MUM ANSWERS
Body: Radiant, healthy, vibrant, strong
Finances: Soaring, abundant, flowing
Relationships: Connected, passionate, loving
Career: Growth, contribution, community
Spirituality: Mother Earth, nature
Love: Light
Life: Activated

Notice how you feel after reading this.

So much more empowering, here are my newly programmed beliefs that my Millionaire Mum self chooses. You're welcome to use them if you like.

BELIEFS OF MILLIONAIRE MUM
Body: My body is a miracle.
Finances: There is always more than enough, the more I have the more I can give.
Relationships: People are amazing.
Career: An opportunity for growth, contribution and connection.
Spirituality: Everything is a cycle and happens in divine timing, even when I don't understand.
Love: Is everywhere and the true celebration. I am loved, loveable and loving.
Life: Is here to be cherished, experienced and enjoyed.

Wow, even after writing that, I feel how far I have come.

Miserable Mum and Millionaire Mum are the same person. Just with a different set of beliefs.

Are you ready to change the way you think the way you feel, and as a result, change the way you act and attract into your life?

Are you ready to be your version of a Millionaire Mum?

The truth is that you are a divine being of the universe who is loved, lovable and loving and you deserve all the abundant goodness possible.

If it sounds too good to be true, just try it on for a little bit, just like a new dress or a pair of shoes. Wear it around the house until it becomes more comfortable. When you go out, put it back in the cupboard until it becomes more comfortable to parade around the shopping centre, social media or school ground in.

You don't have to publish a book about it, but of course, if you fully believed it… YOU COULD!

Your power is in the present moment and each moment you can consciously choose your thoughts.

You can simply uncover and replace the limiting belief with a new one and just like sports, you practise it until you get better at it. You just keep practising. For the rest of your life!

So, it's time to drop the BS.

Stop lying to yourself that you're not good enough, that you don't know how, that life is cruel and hard, that money is evil and people are out to get you, that your success means others failure.

Come back to the truth of presence and the divine intelligent being that you are.

Put your hand on your heart, feel your heartbeat and know you are closer today than you have ever been to the REAL you.

Now that I've busted all those myths and taken out the rubbish, cleaned up my subconscious beliefs and created a new truth for myself, the Millionaire Mum is birthed. Both the book and myself.

I have more time with my family than ever.

I created more income in a weekend than I used to working all year long. I have created financial freedom for myself and my family, I contribute to other family's health and wealth, I have created more resources than ever for my clients. I work less than I EVER have and have a strong supportive team who I delegate to. Which also means I pay them a wage and contribute to their family. I support other conscious business owners and have deep connections with my clients and suppliers. I spend my time with people and I love doing things I love and get to show others how to do the same!

SUMMARY:

- Your internal beliefs = your external life.
- Often, you're not aware of your own beliefs.
- Beliefs either limit you or empower you.
- A belief is a thought and a thought can be changed.
- When I changed my beliefs, my life changed.
- It is easier than you think.

Chapter Seven

MAGIC MORNING ROUTINE: SUPER CHARGE YOUR DAY

"Everything you desire in life will come quicker when you implement and commit to a morning routine."
Diane McKendrick

Yes. EVERYTHING!

- ✔ Lose weight and tone up.
- ✔ Gain more energy and increase your health and fitness.
- ✔ Cultivate more passion and connection in your current relationship.
- ✔ Call in a new relationship.
- ✔ Connect at a deeper level with your children.
- ✔ Manifest or make more money so you can spend more time doing what you love.

After my massive success in the last few years, people constantly ask me, *"Di, how did you do it?"*

They want the silver bullet, the secret strategy… Well, here it is!

My Magic Morning Routine.

Every morning, I take time for ME. I use my morning to anchor myself back to my Soul Purpose, to connect with my intuition, higher self, creator. I move my body in a way that feels good and start my day on purpose.

If I had to choose ONE thing that has had the greatest impact on my sustainable soulful success, it is my Magic Morning Routine (followed closely by EFT tapping – which you can learn more about on my YouTube channel).

Many people disregard the power of a Morning Routine because of its accessibility and simplicity. They would rather pay tens of thousands of dollars to go to a course for someone to tell them how to run their life and be happy.

You have the magic and the answers right at your fingertips.

This concept is not rocket science and definitely not the first time most of you have heard about a morning routine or ritual. Unfortunately, most of you are not committed to time to yourself every morning and spend the first few hours of your day scrolling social media, watching news or sitting in traffic.

Alternatively, a handful of you are attempting a routine but something rigid and outdated that is more of a pain in the butt then something you go to bed the night before excited about! As our iPhones and computers need to be upgraded and updated regularly, so does your morning routine.

The first key is to create something that feels good, and is easy and exciting. When I am doing my go-to-bed routine, I am literally looking forward to waking up in the morning to my magic morning routine. If you're not excited about it and it doesn't feel good, you won't continue to do it. When creating yours, make sure you pick things that you enjoy and feel good.

Regular mistakes and myths people make about morning routines are:

- It needs to be a certain amount of time.
- They get "too" serious and rigid about it.
- They fill it with things Tony Robbins, me or other coaches tell you to do, rather than things that excite YOU and align with YOUR values and purpose.

Many people have a checklist on the fridge or written in their journal and the dialogue they use around their morning routine is along the lines of *"Have To"* or *"Checklist"* or *"Morning Chores."*

When this is the way, it ends up usually being more stress than sustainable and life changing.

I am going to share mine here to get you started, and you can borrow mine until you feel ready to create your own Magic Morning.

Firstly, let's visit the moment we wake up, how we greet the day and create awareness around the part we play and choose when we do the most natural and normal thing for the majority of humans. Wake up each morning.

So, what's your "wake up style?"

1. Alarm
2. No Alarm

Did you choose this consciously or did you just do what you were taught?

Likely what you learnt from your parents or from watching Home and Away or Neighbours.

A few years ago, I decided I didn't want to wake up to an alarm clock anymore. When I visited my personal "wake up style," I realised that the alarm clock startled me and gave me a fright when I woke up. I realised my body reacts better when left to wake up when it is ready.

If I have an event, I will set an alarm clock as a back-up, however I find when I wake up to an alarm, it startles me and then I carry that energy through the day. I have trained my brain to wake me up five minutes before my alarm sounds.

Yes, it works!

Sounds crazy, right? But remember, your subconscious knows the time.

Before I go to bed, when I am setting my phone alarm, I speak to my subconscious and say *"Brain, I command you to wake me up at 5.55am (or 5 minutes before the time I set my alarm for)."*

99% of the time I will wake up to the minute.

I invite you to give this a go. Set the extra alarm just in case, you will be surprised at your own ability to wake up when you want to.

It's time to set and choose your own wake up style.

Ultimately, we have trained our brain to rely on an outside source (alarm clock), even for something as simple as waking up. I realised if I wanted to empower my own life, that I could at least trust myself to WAKE UP when I needed to.

It's time to retrain ourselves to believe in our innate abilities and not be a slave to time and outside influences.

My interpretation of this is: If my first waking moment is from an alarm which startles me from my sleep and is set at a certain time because of an outside event or circumstance, my first waking moment is reactive.

Being directed by outside circumstances job, events, kids whatever it may be. When I dissected the concept and dove deeper, I felt disempowered to outside circumstances. So, I changed it.

I have since designed my life around being able to wake up when I want, when my body feels like it.

Some of you might be thinking, *"Come on girlfriend, come back to the real world! I've got a job and kids to get ready for school, lunches to make, meetings to plan. Ain't no way I can just mosey through my morning, wake up and roll out of bed whenever I want to. I GOT RESPONSIBILITY!"*

YES! I hear you and I know this because this is what I used to (and sometimes still do) think of when people offer information, ideas or concepts that are polarising to the masses of people. My ego goes into overdrive thinking exactly that.

Instead of getting into an argument with the voice in my head, I asked myself, *"What would be the perfect morning for me?"*

Upon answering that question, I designed, refined my wake up style and manifested my Magic Morning Routine and therefore the dream life I desired and now live.

Your Millionaire Mindset (or whatever you are manifesting) starts in the morning, every morning, in your own bed.

Magic Morning Routine: Super Charge Your Day

BEFORE you even open your eyes. Stop handing your power over to outside circumstances, the alarm clock, or whatever you have do that day.

While reading this, I want you to remember this.

The moment you wake is a POWER POINT in your day. The unspoken and unseen feelings, energies, and decisions you consciously or subconsciously choose when you wake up each day will determine the QUALITY OF YOUR LIFE.

Most of you have never paused or been shown how to review your wake up style, and morning routine. This surprises me as I get to witness daily the impact of this process and commitment in mine and my clients' lives.

The moment you wake in the morning is a POWER POINT of your day, all of your days together equal your life so if we can simple change this moment with focused intention, you can:

CHANGE YOUR WHOLE LIFE BY CHANGING WHAT YOU THINK AND DO WHEN YOU WAKE UP.

Once you change what you know about how, when and why you wake up, your life will improve instantly. No extra time, effort, energy, money… Simply awareness.

You are all busy people with lots to do so I don't want to give you more to do and lump you with a lengthy, non-sustainable morning routine. I want to shine awareness on what you are currently doing and how we can tweak and refine it to get you MORE of what you want in life.

No matter how far or deep you are along the journey from Stuck to Seen, there are a few fundamentals I will teach you which will continue to expand with you.

When I was depressed and overweight, I would wake up in the mornings to an alarm BEEP. BEEP! BEEP! Feeling lethargic, fatigued, miserable, I would press snooze several times before eventually dragging myself out of bed.

My first thought used to be, *"I can't wait to go back to bed tonight!"*

I despised myself, I despised life. I never had anything nice to wear, I would complain all day every day about the heat, the news, the weather, work, people. I was miserable. People picked on me and bullied me at work. Boyfriends cheated on me, I was always sick and felt isolated, lonely and defeated. I drove an hour through traffic to a job that sucked my soul dry, listening to the News which as an empath made me feel physically panicked, useless and unworthy.

I was flaky with my commitments, invitations and friendships. Often turning up extremely late. I didn't respect my own time and therefore completely disregarded others' time and talents.

By the time I got to work each day, I was an anxious mess. The worst part of this was - IT WAS NORMAL! I was surrounded by older, bitter miserable people who were also depressed, anxious, and robotic. Like Zombies, eating crap, on medication, depressed, toxic people who were doing their best at life, but like me, had no idea there was another way…

Magic Morning Routine: Super Charge Your Day

Common regular morning thoughts and patterns:

Stuck:

- I feel stuck.
- I am so tired.
- I don't want to get out of bed.
- I can't be bothered.
- I would rather be asleep.

Self-aware:

- Maybe it won't be that bad.
- Listen to something like a podcast or music to feel better.
- Morning musings.

Guilty:

- I can't believe I spent that money on myself.
- I'm not as good as them.
- It's not fair.
- I'm not good enough.
- I don't deserve it.

Focused:

- I've got so much to do today.
- I'm so busy.
- I can't keep up.
- I gotta take meat out for dinner and then I got to drop A to here, pick B up, workout in between.

- Oh, Calendly! I forgot to set my Calendly up. I gotta do that today.

Seen:

- I am open and receptive to all good.
- I love myself.

I know within 2-3 minutes of interaction with someone (online or offline) what their whole life is like by what they tell me happens in the first 30 seconds of waking up each morning.

For example, if you are pressing snooze seven times, I bet you procrastinate ALL day. If you wake up and your first thought is, *"Oh my, I have so much to do today!"*

I'll bet you're overwhelmed. If you wake up like I used to and think, *"I can't do today,"* you're probably depressed. Unless you have already reviewed your wake up style and morning routine - or lack of it.

This is why knowing your values and belief systems is so important for the next part of your life and in creating a sustainable and enjoyable morning experience and therefore LIFE.

The good thing for ALL of you is that you actually already have a morning routine, whether you realise it or not! Now is time to set it up to reflect the new SEEN YOU. It doesn't have to be perfect every time.

Magic Morning Routine: Super Charge Your Day

We practise before perfection and by the time you get it perfected, it will be time to change it again.

Let's uncover what your current morning routine is so we can adapt it to suit the New You.

Include how you wake, what your 1st thought is and your actions for the first 30 minutes.

Example: I wake up to an alarm set at the same time every day. I press snooze a few times before rolling out of bed without much thought and shuffle to the bathroom. Go to the loo. Wash my hands, avoiding the mirror. Thank God the kids are still asleep, so I can drink my coffee in peace. Then I head straight out to the kitchen where I put the kettle on, turn the news on and eat my Weetbix. Sometimes I sit at the table or often in the garden in my egg chair. I scroll Facebook while I eat and listen to the birds. When I walk back inside, I notice the mess everywhere, and pick up a few things, then make lunches. I make my second coffee, help the kids get ready and then I'm off to work for the day.

Your turn!

Share your CURRENT Morning Routine below. NOTE: be as specific as you can:

_____

_____

_____

_____

_____

DISCLAIMER: Once you dissect your current morning routine and implement the tips and tricks in this chapter and book, your life *will* take off. As with anything, what goes up must come down.

I call it "landing." As you start to fly and upgrade your connections, beliefs, values, morning routines and actions, naturally you will soar. So, we need to ensure you upgrade your "landing gear," otherwise you come down crashing down with a hard, painful thump.

I used my morning routine to upgrade my landing gear and come back to land and ground each morning, regardless of how high I fly through the day. The morning is a time for coming home to yourself. To anchor back into your truth and presence.

CREATE YOUR MAGIC MORNING ROUTINE

Now it's time to actually consciously CHOOSE your wake-up style and morning routine each morning. We do this by getting super clear about how we want our life to look and feel in five or ten years from now.

Magic Morning Routine: Super Charge Your Day

Your compelling new identity, the new YOU.

The SEEN you.

The one who is fit, healthy, flexible, the one who has a loving relationship with mutual respect, clear boundaries. The Millionaire or financially free you, the awakened, connected and spirited YOU. What would she think and do when she first wakes up? She is there, ready and waiting with your answers, you just have to ask her and listen.

My Magic Morning Routine:

I let my body wake naturally with the cycle of the sun. This is usually between 4:30am and 6am. If she is tired she sleeps longer, if she is rested she wakes early. As my body moves from my night time sleep into twilight, I begin to wake and subconsciously prepare for the freedom of my day. As I gently open my eyes, I look at the ceiling and do a gratitude rampage. A random amount of time that feels good and I run through all that I am grateful for. I stand up and outstretch my arms saying internally, *"I am open and receptive to all good."*

I plant my feet on the floor and feel the grounding to the earth. I am grateful, again. As I slowly at a pace that feels comfortable move towards the bathroom, I chant a song in my head. At the moment it is, *"I love myself, just the way I am. There is nothing I need to change, I will always be the perfect me. There is nothing to rearrange."* It's a song I learnt at my very first personal development workshop many moons ago.

After going to the toilet, I get dressed straight away. My gym gear on the floor set out the night before ready to get into immediately. I put it on, not thinking about whether or not I want to walk to just focusing on the present moment. I walk to the kitchen and turn on the kettle. Walk to the coffee machine and switch her on (once again the coffee has been prepared the night before) so it's easy and the press of the button.

While the coffee machine warms up, I head over to the mirror and do my mirror work, *"Diane. I love you, I really, really love you."*

Connect in. Go deeper. Feeling full and confident, I walk to my white board and review my Soul Purpose and FEEL IT. I then look over my nurturing funnel, my numbers and I thank them. I remind myself. 1 million dollars a year is only $83k a month, $19k a week and $3k a day.

I lay my eyes of the $500k goal and decide that's my next step. I am closer to that. It seems more real. I remind myself. The amount of money is irrelevant, its already there waiting for me, once I hit the vibration of that amount it will present itself.

I walk back to the coffee machine and get my black coffee in my take away mug which once again is arranged ready and waiting the night before.

I head off for my morning walk. Listen to my morning musing, drink my coffee, listen to the birds. I go the same way every day so I don't have to think.

Magic Morning Routine: Super Charge Your Day

I tune into my body and ask, *"How do you feel today? What do you need today?"*

I answer myself.

Once I recognise how my body feels, I honour it. I decide what I will do for the next 20-40-minute walk. The walk is slow and gentle.

Sometimes I do EFT tapping, sometimes I do my walking meditation (get a FREE copy from Spotify: Those 2 Sisters Meditations) and often I'll just wander and watch the birds and horses and marvel at the magic of the sunrise. Sometimes I will share a FB post and reply to messages, some days I cry the whole way, and most mornings I'll do a quick and inspiring Insta story.

Every now and again, the kids come with me and it's chaotic, constant chatter and a million questions. Sometimes they ask, and I say, *"NO."*

Particularly on the mornings where I need the quiet and time to myself.

When I get back, I stand in the sun and do my back exercises to counteract the amount of time I spend sitting at the computer, I do my morning breathing exercises and finish off with gratitude and then picking three goals and visualizing them as though they are done.

As mentioned in the beginning of the book, your brain doesn't know the difference between a vivid imagination and a real-time memory, so I visualise my goals with intense emotion as though it's already true. I then look around my current life and duplicate and enhance that emotion with what I already have.

Seems like a lot? All this is done in usually less than 40- 45 minutes. I set my state before I walk back in the door to my home to be present and focused with the family. My phone goes away and that leaves space for sacred time where we eat, discuss, and get ready for our day together. When the kids were smaller, they would sit on my lap but now they play, bicker, get ready for school, ask me to brush their hair and fight over lost socks and library bags.

I rarely book any events or calls before 9am so I can spend the sacred time with my family enjoying the time together without the stress of a deadline. Obviously, we have to get out the door for school drop but if we are late. I have learnt not to stress over it as it won't change it. Once I discovered this, magically enough I stopped being late. Go figure!

About ten years ago (back when I was still pressing snooze 15 times a morning), I did the process I am getting you to do with this chapter. Checking with my future self and asking her what my mornings would look like. My brain told me it was impossible, and I would never stick with it. I wasn't smart or disciplined enough to see it through. I figured I had to do something every morning, so it might as well be the things that made me feel good.

However, after committing to and completing the process that is offered in this book that you are completing and reading about right now, I created the above.

Magic Morning Routine: Super Charge Your Day

My morning routine is non-negotiable, it is set in alignment with my goals, values and beliefs. Even when I travel or on holidays, I love it so much I still do it. Every. Single. Day

Obviously depending what is going on I often have to adapt it but it is very similar most days.

I want to help you create and connect with yours so it's something you look forward to every single day. Don't just duplicate mine, go deeper.

Ask your future self what she would do and honour where you are at.

For example, if she says, walk every day and you have achy joints and a knee problem, DON'T start with doing a walk. Adapt it to light gentle movement that supports your healing.

If you aren't a morning person, don't force yourself to get up at 4:30am. Be kind to yourself and get up a little later. The magic is in the alignment of your beliefs and values. If you are still in a job but plan to start your own business, add that into your routine.

This isn't my first rodeo and I know from the past that only about 50% of you will actually complete the above process and even less, probably about 5% will implement it and less again will continue it. Maybe 2% of you will still be doing it in a year.

With growth being one of my highest values, I started to question as to why some people did it and others didn't.

Lucky for you, I found the answer which means we could have a 100% strike rate here.

The determining factor is: If you value your health and wellbeing, you will do it. If you don't, you won't! So now it's my job to teach you and remind you of your own self-worth, which in theory, means 100% of you will complete this and maintain it! BOOM!

Most of us have been programmed to rely on things outside of us for validation, so we take the easy road. We have also been programmed to react instead of create, and that shows by how many people rely on an alarm to wake them. The easiest most natural thing we all do every day. When we use an alarm, the trust in our own self is robbed from us every morning.

Society sets us up to consume, instead of create.

If you are reading this book and you have got this far, you are a CREATOR. You are ready for the next step and it's only the story you're telling yourself about why you can't have the life of your dreams; the fear that is stopping you from getting it.

You have been programmed to give up when it gets hard. Our morning routine is a chance to put a laser on all these big embedded belief systems that have been created from our culture or society and say YES to what works for us and NO to what doesn't; instead of reacting to the programming.

If you can master your morning, you WILL master your life.

Magic Morning Routine: Super Charge Your Day

The state you set for the day will infuse through your life, finances, relationships, ideas, and interactions. EVERYTHING.

So, what are you waiting for? Go and get started!

SUMMARY:

- Everything you desire in life will come quicker when you implement and commit to a morning routine.

- People want to know the magic bullet to my success - Magic Morning Routine hands down!

- A morning routine is used to anchor you back to your soul purpose, to connect with your intuition, higher self, creator. To move your body in a way that feels good and start your day on purpose.

- A good morning routine is easy and accessible, not dependant on income or age.

- It's important to create a routine that feels good to you and that you enjoy.

- You all have a current "wake up style, morning routine and 1st thought" You can consciously choose yours instead of just patterning what you learnt from your parents or from TV programs.

- Alarm clocks are scary.

- Your subconscious can be your new alarm clock.

- Create YOUR routine that is aligned with your values and purpose.

Magic Morning Routine: Super Charge Your Day

- The moment you wake is a POWER POINT in your day. Your thoughts, feelings and actions when you wake will determine the quality of your life.

- Once you implement and stay committed to your morning routine your life will "take off" Therefore you will need to upgrade your landing gear.

- Sacred time with my family each morning is a non-negotiable for me.

- You will only stick with a morning routine if you value your health and wellbeing.

- If you can Master your morning you WILL master your life.

Chapter Eight

MANIFESTING MAGICIAN: FIND YOUR MAGIC

"You are powerful beyond belief and now it is your turn to fully receive."
Diane McKendrick

I'm often fondly referred to as *"The Manifesting Queen"* by friends and family. Funnily enough, it's something I now do so naturally now that I forget it's even a thing. I forget that most people haven't even heard of manifesting and even if you have heard of it, it may be a very new concept to you.

It is my intention that by the end of this chapter, you will have a deep understanding of manifesting on a multi-dimensional scale. Included in this book are tools, strategies, examples and support so you can take this concept and information and manifest absolute magic throughout your entire life.

This chapter will amplify and magnify your manifesting skills and talents, regardless if you are a very beginner, at rock bottom, an experienced manifestor or simply want to dip your toes in and see what this is all about.

As with most things, the more you do it, the better you get!

The good news is... You are already doing it!

Yes, by reading this book, you are already manifesting. Regardless of your awareness, commitment, and understanding, you have manifested this moment. With this book in your hands, and the connection with me; whether our bond is online, in person at an event, through my clothing or jewellery line, retreats, or podcasts.

At some point, consciously or subconsciously, you wanted more from life.

You had a passing thought (or a continuous one) that you are ready to change.

Ready for more in life. Ready to read something, hear something, meet someone that can guide you on the journey. And here we are!

It's time to fly! To be seen, to be heard, to be acknowledged. To take your life to the next level.

Everything in your life right now is manifested, including this moment you have created.

The problem is that most of us are doing it without realising it. One of the laws of the universe is what you hold in constant thought, will express itself outwards.

Most people, the masses, wander around on auto-pilot, complaining about almost everything. Sick and tired of life, hating their job, not enough money, partner's a pain in the butt…

But, guess what?

When they continue to think and say those things, they get more of it. Effectively, they are manifesting the things that make them miserable into their life.

Most people are more comfortable being miserable in a pattern or story they know, even if it's painful, simply because they are familiar with it.

Change is scarier to most so many people are still subconsciously choosing to continue to manifest misery.

We are powerful, expressive and creative beings and unfortunately, most (unless they know better) are "Miserable Manifesting," instead of "Magic Manifesting."

When I first learnt the above, it was extremely confronting.

The person who told me nearly got a fist to the nose! Hahahaha - just kidding.

But I do remember thinking, *"Eurgh! What a do-gooder! It's alright for her, she's got money, a good job, she's fit and healthy. A beautiful husband who would do anything for her. She has no idea what it feels like to have chronic fatigue, drink every night, fight and crawl through traffic for an hour and a half every day to a job that sucks the soul dry and feel lonely and trapped with no way out! How dare she tell me that I manifested the misery in my life, this is NOT my fault! It's THEIR fault!"*

She told me, *"If you can organise your thoughts, you can organise your life. It's an inside job."*

As I started to learn more and understand the science and spirituality behind the concept of manifestation, I realised that in fact, I had created that miserable life for myself. Not intentionally, of course.

It was an indirect response to feeling fundamentally flawed, like there was something wrong with me and that I was useless. Feeling like I didn't deserve anything better, or in fact that there was a possibility of something better.

The first thing to understand, quite simply is - whatever you think about, you get.

Unfortunately, due to trauma or injected belief systems, ideas or fears, many of you unknowingly create numerous layers, stories and excuses of why you can't have what you desire. This is greatly similar to me when I was manifesting my misery in my life.

I finally got to a point where as a result of my unconscious thought processes. I hit a brick wall, which shut me off to the possibility of a better way of life. As I slipped deeper down into the darkness, I became numb. Getting disappointed or let down too many times and no longer daring to dream.

It was too painful to be reminded constantly I wasn't worthy of the magic I saw in other people's lives. So, I shut off to it, turning to alcohol, social media, and TV to distract and numb me.

Your recurring thoughts penetrate your dreams and block your full potential.

Some of you are well aware of this and others of you reading this are still in full denial mode, or perhaps it's the 1st time you have heard something like this and it's a bit of a wakeup call.

If you want a different life, recognise and change your recurring thought into more alignment of the life you desire.

There is a little bit of unpacking we need to do, prior to revealing to you my Magic Manifesting Formula.

Otherwise it will be another thing you have read or learnt, and it gets lost in the excitement and buzz of "self-improvement." This life-changing formula will end up shoved into the cupboard that is already overflowing with old workshop books, post it notes sticking out of them, handwritten scribbled notes on every page, pages folded down and ear marked with your great intention of coming back to re-visit, re-read, or re-type your notes.

Or is it just me with that cupboard? Maybe yours is a drawer?

The day I actually STARTED being present and completing the exercises recommended to me in the books and workshops I spent time reading or attending - my life started to change.

Prior to that, I was always rushing off for the next "self-development fix" to keep filling the empty space inside of me. I was being distracted by the idea of Personal Development and not actually consuming and implementing the course's content. I was just overly focused on "finishing the book" or "completing the course" so I could move onto the next one.

How many of you have got this far and not done the exercises yet?

Or have half assed it, answering a few of the questions and then thinking, *"This is too hard,"* or *"I don't know,"* or getting distracted by work or the kids each time there is an exercise.

Mmmm… Yes, I see you!

Let me just say this. It's kinda like trying to get fit by sitting on the couch and just reading about it. Or trying to find the man of your dreams and literally not talking to any men.

It's just not going to happen.

Now, this chapter is about the magic of manifesting and if you have ever read or heard anything about manifesting, you may be thinking, *"What if I sit on the couch and visualise my healthy fit body? Or imagine being with the man of my dreams? Does that count?"*

Likely you have watched that video on You Tube or read that book which tells you, *"Visualise and hold the vision of the thing you want. Imagine what it will look and feel like and if you do it hard enough for long enough, it will appear."*

This is what most people think manifesting is. Granted, this is an important part of the process but there is so much more to the process overall.

The biggest myth about manifesting is by "IMAGINING" or "VISUALISING" something, it magically pop up in your life.

Visualising is only a small portion of the strategy and one that most coaches or courses will teach you. Many people get disheartened because they are doing exactly that. Imagining REAL HARD but it doesn't happen for them.

Alternatively, it happens for a few of the easier, closer manifestations but when we call in the bigger more elaborate manifestations, it seems to stagnate. We sit and scratch our head and wonder why it's not happening.

Why?

Because it needs to be followed up by inspired action and several other steps that most people either don't know - or couldn't be bothered doing.

My tried-and-tested personal formula gives you a wholesome approach which will fast track and improve your results.

DISCLAIMER: It is important that you know this about me. I promote and subscribe to sustainable, maintainable results, outcomes and growth.

Not the one-hit-wonder where you do an $80k month in sales for your online business ONCE and then spend the rest of your life on social media trying to prove to yourself and your clients you have a million-dollar business.

Not the yo-yo, fad dieting or fitness challenges where you lose 20kg in a challenge and then spend the next 6 months putting back on 40kg and feel like a loser and even more ashamed and embarrassed in your own skin.

Not the morning routine which lasts for three weeks and then you go back to hitting snooze 15 times before rolling your sore, sorry body out of bed.

Not the roundabout of dating "good enough" men or women who don't meet your criteria and you constantly renegotiate your boundaries. Where you sacrifice your values and self-care for someone else.

Not the relationship that looks picture perfect on Social Media but then you both go to bed with an empty, sick feeling in your stomach feeling so incredibly lonely and trapped.

I am committed to getting myself and therefore, YOU, sustainable, long term results.

To quietly and diligently keep creating content, merchandise, community, teaching, educating, inspiring and empowering YOU to raise the standard of your life so these things that you once dreamed of and manifested become your normal life.

To raise the quality of your life one area, one day, one moment at a time to give you a solid sturdy foundation to continue to create and build upon.

To help connect you back to your Soul Guided Purpose so you can leave a legacy and make a difference in this world.

If you like the sound of that… Read on! If you don't like the sound of that, read on anyway!

I am about to reveal my secret formula, but first we need to get clear on your starting point.

Read through the table below and tick who and where you are NOW.

Millionaire Mum

MANIFESTING MILESTONES
WHERE ARE YOU IN YOUR MANIFESTING JOURNEY?

CURRENT AWARENESS	DESCRIPTION	MILESTONE	WHO ARE YOU NOW?
NO IDEA ISABELLE (Stuck)	You've never heard of manifesting before and thought it was some kind of disease you caught whilst swimming in the Bremer River. Or you have heard what manifesting is and think it's ridiculous. If you mentioned it to your friendship group, they'd throw a cream bun at you and wonder if you'd start "drinking the coolaid."	Asleep, disconnected and stuck.	
DOING IT DAILY DEBBIE (Self-aware/ Guilty)	You've heard of manifesting before through books and podcasts. You're exploring the idea and playing around with manifesting minor daily things. You're starting to talk about it more in your friendship group and wondering if you can really do it. You've briefly mentioned it to your friendship group, and they're a little curious and want to learn more; although they'll rather sit back and watch before giving it a try.	Starting to manifest small daily things which you believe are; 1. Easy 2. Accessible 3. Believable 4. Possible EXAMPLE: Green lights and car parks	
STAYING SAFE SALLY (Fully Focused)	You've had some positive experience with manifesting daily things and have decided to up the ante to really test if it works. You're starting to explore more important things to manifest whilst keeping positive and safe. You're still conscious of how it might all look and sound to some people. You've mentioned your friendship group for a while now, and they give you a knowing nod and smile. They share their latest manifesting story and encourage you to take your next step.	Starting to manifest bigger things which you believe are: 1. Possible but risky 2. A stretch for you 3. Uncomfortable 4. A big jump EXAMPLE: New car, certain amount of money for something, a holiday, new job, computer, dream partner	
DREAMING WILDLY DIANA (seen)	You've manifested the possible and safe things in your life and are now wondering what else is out there for you. You now have a whole community who supports and believes in you. You have a deep knowing that you're on the right path and living your Soul Guided Mission and your manifestations are often in contribution to serving a bigger purpose. When mentioning this to your friendship group, you feel vulnerable and exposed. They respond with love, support and gratitude and cheer you on the whole way.	Starting to manifest even bigger things which you believe are: 1. Impossible 2. Petrifying 3. Seems so far away 4. Out of your league EXAMPLE: Writing a book about being a millionaire before you are one, your dream house by the beach, your own aeroplane	

Now you have your starting point, go to www.dianemckendrick to do the Manifesting Magician Module in the Mastermind. It's FREE for 7 days!

One last thing before we get started.

Always remember when doing any type of manifesting to speak in the present tense as though it has already happened and add the vibration of gratitude for it already having happened.

Now you know where you are and where you want to be, you understand speaking in the present tense as though it has already happened…

It's time for me to spill the beans and give you my secret formula.

Gratitude + Present Tense =
Magic Manifesting

DIANE MCKENDRICKS MANIFESTING MAGICIAN FORMULA

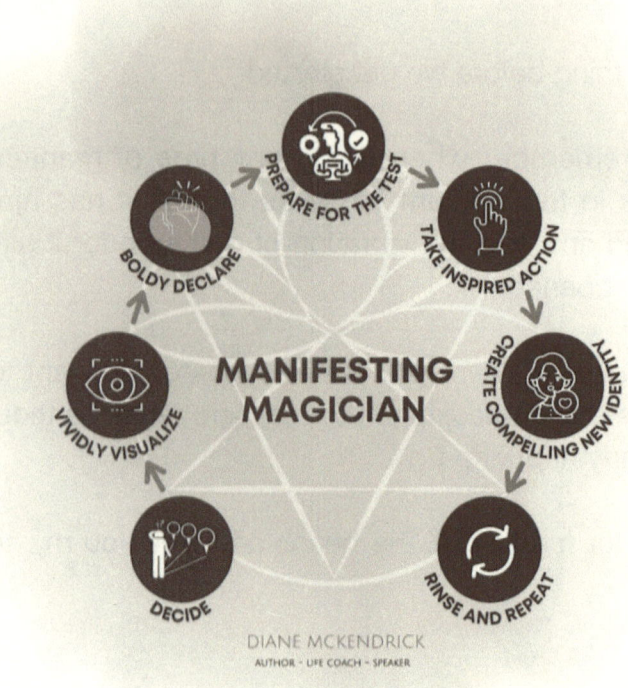

DECIDE: Be specific! Decide EXACTLY what you are manifesting. Be clear and precise so there is no question as to what you are manifesting.

Once you have got clear and made your specific decision, ask yourself, *"What is the feeling this thing will give me?"*

Example: If you are manifesting more income, pick an exact amount. Instead of saying *"I want more income,"* trying saying, *"I am grateful for my $1000 pay rise, I feel so acknowledged for my service I provide daily and it provides security for myself and my family."*

VIVIDLY VISUALISE: Hold in your mind the visualisation of this event, experience, occurrence unfolding. How will you feel? What will it look like? Who is around you? Add all your senses. What can you hear, what can you smell? What clothes are you wearing? What is your location?

Example: When I manifested publishing my first book, *"Rise Up, The Soulful Guide to Success,"* I would wake up ten minutes early every day and imagine being at an event with hundreds of people, signing it and handing it out. I imagined a line of people waiting to speak to me and purchase the book. I imagined receiving testimonials of photos with things ear marked, highlighted and underlined with handwritten notes of the page. Messages from people saying that the book had changed their life.

I literally dropped myself in that moment in the future and lived it and felt it like it was NOW. This was long before I had even written one word of my book.

BOLDLY DECLARE: Declare it BOLDLY and INTENSELY to the universe. Create an action, statement or expression which declares your Magic Manifestation to the universe.

Example: Write a book about being a millionaire before you are one. Do a presale for your product before finishing it. Declare your intention to your friends and family.

PREPARE FOR THE TEST: Something will happen either discrete or in your face to see if you are REALLY ready to receive your manifestation. Watch for this so it doesn't blindside you.

Example: If you are manifesting a fit, healthy, strong body and want to lose weight, maybe you will get sick or be put into many situations where there is lots of junk food enticing and testing your resolution.

TAKE INSPIRED ACTION: Implement small action steps daily to move you closer.

Example: If you are manifesting a partner, clean out his side of the garage for his car to fit, make space on his side of the bed for him to put his slippers.

When I was writing my first book, I cleared space in my office to store 500 copies of my book.

When I was manifesting having children I bought a few baby singlets and washed them and hung them on my clothes line between our clothes. Blue first and then pink. That's the way it worked out for us.

CREATE A COMPELLING NEW IDENTITY
The Old You doesn't know how to be the new version of you. Left unsupervised, these parts of yourself with clash. Who you thought you once were, fighting against who it is you are in this moment of manifestation. In order to come to peace with who and where you are at the moment, we need to create the Compelling New YOU and integrate it with the past.

Example: Visit Mastermind to complete and connect to your compelling new identity: Masterclass.

RINSE & REPEAT
This manifestation has now become your normal, everyday life and now it's time to Level Up again. Return to step one and REPEAT step by step.

Now you have my secret formula, you can manifest anything your heart desires into your world. Trust the process, share your WINS on my Personal Facebook page Diane McKendrick.

Keep practising and being amazed at your own absolute power.

The more you do this, the better you get. Share the formula with your friends, family and colleagues and help others tap into their infinite power within.

You are powerful beyond belief and now it is your turn to fully receive.

Simply follow the steps above to show yourself the internal power that has been locked inside of you for far too long. Even when things get tough, even on the hard days, this magic resides inside of you. Take a moment now to fully feel the magnificence that is YOU!

Do not move onto the next chapter until you have completed all the exercises. Even if it takes a day or two. The tools, videos, spreadsheets, diagrams over there in the Mastermind have been designed from my heart to yours.

SUMMARY:

- Manifesting is multidimensional, powerful and everyone does it.

- You are already doing it, everything in your life right now, including this moment you have created. Most of us are doing it without realising it.

- The masses (most people) unknowing manifest misery. This can be confronting to accept that you have created your current reality. Particularly if it is painful or traumatic.

- We are powerful expressive and creative beings and our thoughts express themselves outwards.

- If you can organise your thoughts, you can organise your life. Start on the inside.

- Many people will manifest miserable life, unknowingly as a response to feeling fundamentally flawed, like something is wrong with them. An intrinsic feeling of uselessness and worthlessness.

- What you think about you get.

- Unresolved trauma or injected belief systems, ideas or fear create layers, stories and excuses of why you can't have what you desire.

- Your recurring thoughts penetrate your dreams and block your full potential. If you want a different life, recognise and change your recurring thought into more alignment of the life you desire.

- The exercises in this book won't work unless you DO them.

- Manifestations need to be followed up by focused intention and inspired action.

- Just sitting on the couch visualising might work for the simple things but there is more to the formula which most of you won't be bothered to do.

- I promote and subscribe to sustainable, maintainable results, outcomes and growth.

- It's my mission to remind and connect you back to your Soul Guided purpose so you can leave a legacy and make a difference in this world. To show you how to build a sturdy foundation to continue to create and build upon.

- This formula works best if you know your starting point (visit dianemckendrick.com) to complete the Manifesting Magician Module mastermind.

- Manifesting works best when you speak in the present tense as though it has already happened and add the vibration of gratitude for it already having happened.

- Gratitude + Present Tense = Magic Manifesting

Chapter Nine

ABSOLUTE ABUNDANCE

"Abundance is a frequency, a beautiful contagious frequency. The more you have, the more you get. The more you get, the more you give. The more you give, the more you get!"
Diane McKendrick

If you're reading this book, it's because you want more out of life, right?

You are probably a mother in business or craving something more from life. Perhaps wanting to start your own business, or contribute to your family financially. Regardless of being a parent or not, many people are spending a lot of time doing uninspiring tasks. Busy as you have ever been and doing a lot but not getting much done.

Regardless of where you are in your developmental stages from Stuck, Self-Aware, Guilty, Focused or Seen, most people's dominant state is one of burnout and feeling exhausted and overwhelmed.

Working hard or hardly working - having one area of your life skyrocket while the others seem to explode in a flame of glory and dismantle themselves before your eyes and end up in tatters at your feet.

You see something in my life that you desire for yours.

The feedback I get from many of you, current clients, followers or fan girls (lol) that you are wondering how I do it all. Motherhood, sacred business, fit, flexible body, connected relationships, finances, friendships.

Millionaire Mum… How does she do it? Is she some rainbow unicorn who frolics across the fairy floss plains into the sunset? Is this possible for me?

That's Di, she's different. It's easy for her. Her husband is amazing, and her kids are happy. Everything she touches turns to gold.

You need to know, as with everything, this is just a 'part truth.' The full truth encompasses both sides.

What most of you and social media don't see is the years of pain and trauma I experienced in leading me to this life.

What you don't see is the hours of work I put in around the clock. What you don't see is the hundreds and thousands of dollars I have spent on healings, seminars, books, courses, and mentorships.

What you don't see is the black hole depressed days and how hard I am on myself to show up and serve and support the community. The voice in my head that constantly tells me to feel worthy I have to overachieve. To overdeliver. The insatiable drive for growth, bigger goals, more impact. To reduce suffering because I can, and I know how, but feeling broken and sad when the people who need the work the most, are not interested.

I designed this woman. I created her.

All parts of her and her life-long mission is to continue to accept and nurture all parts of her. The good, the bad, the ugly.

The understanding that I am ALL of the things cultivates a sense of wholeness and peace.

I don't attach to the perceived 'good' side anymore and have stopped hiding or pretending that the perceived "bad" side does not exist. They co-inhabit my human body working together, arguing, challenging each other and ultimately, like a never-ending tug of war. Just like siblings who love each other but bicker most of the time. Poking and prodding.

People speak of abundance mostly in the realm of money.

My interpretation of abundance is a wholesome approach to ALL areas of life and understanding they all intertwined together.

True abundance to me isn't the amount of money in the bank account or the number on the scales. It's not determined by the number of followers or monthly sales. It's not the car, the house, the clothes you wear.

ABSOLUTE abundance is the way you feel each morning when you wake up.

Waking up on purpose with a deep sense of self and connection that holds you accountable to yourself. Defining and refining your Soul Purpose so you can design your day and life around it, the spring in my step, the sparkle in my eye, the friendships, connections, coffee dates, cacao catch ups, health, and fitness.

A feeling of gratitude and celebration every morning I wake up because of mundane, daily things that I get to experience and do.

The acceptance and embracing of all parts of myself and life.

Absolute abundance is NOT in the future; it is in the NOW. The present moment.

Absolute Abundance

Abundance is a frequency, a beautiful contagious frequency. The more that you have, the more you get. The more that you get, the more that you give. The more you give, the more you get!

YOU GET TO CHOOSE.

Abundance seems to be buzzwords out there in the overly ambitious Personal Development world at the moment. I invite you to take a moment and tune into what abundance is to YOU.

What does it look and feel like to you?

When do you know you have it?

Can you flick it on like a switch?

Where do you feel it in your body?

I have cracked the code, opened the floodgates of absolute abundance for myself and then therefore for others in my community. And let me tell you… IT FEELS GRAND!

Once again, the good news is that you don't have to be, do or have anything outside of yourself to experience abundance.

It is within you. YES! YOU, right now!

Try this. Close your eyes and take a big deep breath. Notice how the air is there for you? As much and as often as you like.

YES. This is one of those exercises that I actually expect you to stop, put the book down and do.

If you haven't done it yet, stop and take a deep breath.

And again, deeper this time.

Notice how the more you ask for the more there is.

Well, that is the characteristic of abundance. Ask, believe and you shall receive! It's there waiting for you to ask for it, to invite it in. To expand and embody Absolute Abundance.

Simply flick on the "Abundance Switch."

Take time to tune into what is already there for you that you take for granted:

- Oxygen
- Digestion
- Nature

List below the abundance that is already there for you which you haven't noticed:

_____

_____

_____

_____

_____

I used to think it was something outside of me that I have to chase down. That I had to earn. I had to work for it. I associated abundance with deservedness and because I had low self-worth, I didn't deserve the good things in life. Not only did I not deserve the good things in life, but I was exempt from any type of abundance because I was unworthy.

I know now that is not the truth and the truth is abundance is a vibration and it's available to me and YOU right now in this moment. A frequency; a choice.

One million dollars is a vibration and when I match that internally, the external world will reflect it.

My healthy weight is a vibration and when I match that on the inside, my body reflects it outwardly.

- Health, same thing
- Relationships, same thing
- Business, same thing
- Finances, same again!

I remember my first experience of this is when I set my income target for a $60k month.

Immediately (and every day), my brain told me it was impossible; looking at the numbers it was impossible. My brain didn't know how. So, I acknowledged it and let it go, dropped back into my heart and trusted.

Previously, I would have started pounding the pavement, doing more work, creating new products, making sales calls, running events. This time I decided I would invest that time effort and energy on FEELING what $60k a month felt like.

Tuning in every day to how the vibration of $60k a month felt. I then took a moment to compare the feeling of a $20k (which I had already experienced) to $60k - and surprise, surprise, it felt different.

The focused intention and inspired action I did take then came from a $60k a month vibration instead of the $20k a month vibration. This created massive momentum and impact.

Please know that this invisibility infuses into all areas of your life. This is an example of how this works and if I wasn't as aware and committed to this work, it could have been a very different outcome.

My high-viber, multi-million-dollar business friends asked me to go on a girls trip to Port Douglas with them and my first thoughts were, *"No, I don't have time for it, these ladies are millionaires so they will probably stay somewhere expensive and I can't afford that. They have more money than me. I'll be the odd one out. What if they meet me and don't like me? What if they choose ridiculously expensive restaurants and I can't go?"*

Without too much more thought, I replied to the message:

"Thanks so much for thinking of me, but I can't go this time round. Have fun!"

After about a minute of hitting "reply" and sending this message back, I observed my thoughts, and asked myself, "What would my $60k per month vibration self do?"

Well, she would go, of course! So, I sent back another message:

"That answer came from my old identity and belief system. My new identity says GO. So, I'm in, what are the dates? Let's book this baby!"

After booking flights (my first Qantas flight in 11 years - I have been blessed with getting staff travel with Virgin for over a decade) and discussing booking accommodation, the idea was booking ourselves separate rooms so we could have our own space another massive jump for me!

In the past when I travelled, I always stayed at backpackers or was the one trying to sneak more people into the room to split the cost to "save money."

Although I had said YES to the trip, I was still unknowingly stuck in an old scarcity mindset.

I had convinced myself it was resourceful and it was a clever way of being able to justify the trip. Our brain is pretty clever at tricking us when we are transitioning. I looked up and found some local backpackers for $20 a night and was about to send the text to my friends to let them know I had decided to stay at the backpackers to save money and just meet my friends at the resort pool daily.

Millionaire Mum

Committed to my $60k month manifestation, I again asked, *"What would my $60k per month self do?"*

The answer came. She would book her own room, close to her friends so she could have her own space but company when she desired it. The simplicity and efficiency of having a room at the resort is your value. How much do you value your time that will be spent organising Ubers, food, packing to stay out for the whole day?

I decided not only my own room, but one of the nicest in the resort would be my choice for this trip. So, I booked.

Now I had four days booked away in a 5-star hotel with some really amazing women. Bookings were finalised, payments were made, and I thought, *"Hey, it's smooth sailing from here!"*

Without realising, I was running a guilt pattern, in order to feel worthy of taking this trip I had convinced myself that the trip was dedicated to "writing my book" so I set about making the trip about writing my book instead of relaxing and doing nothing. I couldn't possibly go away and do nothing for four days, could I?

I was so busy in the lead up to the trip, with events, family and work that I didn't really have another chance to think of it until 10pm the night before. I held a massive event the night before and at 10pm when I got home, I thought, *"Better pack for tomorrow!"*

Hahahaha, well this is how I live my life. I'm still not sure if this is my $20k self or $60k self. I will let you know when I work it out! It's always a work in progress...

I noticed as soon as I started to pack, the guilt creeping in. Because of the event the night before, I was home late, left early so didn't see my husband or kids in the evening or the morning. I left, and I was going away for four days. I left my house at 5am and cried. A deep sense of guilt, grief and uncertainty. Especially with the world epidemic we had all just endured and was in the middle of.

I picked up my friend and we rocked up to the airport super early and the emotional avalanche blindsided me, and completely caught me off guard. As I walked through the Qantas terminal, I realised it was the first time since Gus lost his job with Virgin that I had been to the airport. The first time since the Coronavirus pandemic that I had been out in the greater public space.

It felt different. People were different. I was different.

This was the first time in 10 years I had paid full price for a flight. The emotions all hit me at once and I had another reality check that my husband had lost his job, his identity, his soul purpose, our family's income and therefore, security. That the world had changed and so many people in a state of depression, loss and despair and here I was off, swanning around the countryside on a girls' weekend.

With my laptop on my shoulder, I patted it thinking, *"Not a girls' weekend, a writing weekend."*

For some reason, this made me feel better.

I enjoyed the plane trip and was settled by the afternoon in the 5-star resort. Nestled up at the swim up bar with the sun setting, nowhere to be and nothing to do, except relax and be with my friends.

Here, I had the biggest ah ha moment.

At the time, Ross was eight and Esme was six. It's not unusual for me to go away for a few days here and there and I have definitely spent a week or two away from the family during National and International Speaking Tours.

I am also a MASTER at dissolving and neutralising guilt, fear, judgement, resentment in my life so the guilt masked itself skilfully.

However, this was the 1st time I was going to be away for an extended period of time WITHOUT WORKING. To relax, sit by the pool, read books, talk to my friends, have fancy dinners out, beach walks, morning coffees which turned into midday massages, sunset cocktails, endless hours lazing by the pool, moonlight dancing on the beach and basically relaxing for four days.

Once again, without realising my pattern emerged. I was vaguely aware of it but didn't realise how much it affected me until that moment. My brain engaged me in a dialogue that basically could NOT see the value in sitting around and doing nothing for four days.

No plans, no work, nothing scheduled, we didn't even have to cook a meal for ourselves.

What the heck was I going to do for four days?

At that moment, I made a decision. If I felt like writing I would. If I felt like swimming, I would. If I wanted to go stay at the backpackers, I would. If I wanted to go for dinner, I would. If I'd rather stay in my room and read, I would. If I felt like having a sleep, I would. If I wanted a cocktail, I would.

For many years, I thought the fancy 5-star accommodation, expensive dinners, designer clothes were a reflection of abundance and when I could "afford" it, I would feel wealthy.

In that moment, I realised it's not the things at all.

It's the FREEDOM of CHOICE to CHOOSE what YOU genuinely desire in that moment.

The capacity and ability to understand your own values and what's important to you and the FREEDOM to choose! The awareness to choose from the present moment and not from past programming, fear and trauma; which is how the human brain is designed to operate! The default program for us is FEAR.

What if we CHOSE love and abundance as our default?

Abundance is here for us people. All around us. Waiting for us to meet it but too many of us are stuck in the story, excuses and programming to meet it.

And yes, I did make the $60k month. Just as I had visualised every morning in my manifesting. I was sitting at the swim up bar with my friends. The sun was setting and they all had a cocktail. I had water (just like I visualised every morning since setting the goal) and they asked me about business. I got to cheers and celebrate my first ever $66k sales month with my friends from the pool in Port Douglas, drinking water, watching the sun go down.

A big lesson was learnt that day.

Abundance is here for me. Always. I just have to ask, nurture myself to the vibration and it will be provided. Just like the air we breathe.

It feels good; however, I deeply feel the true celebration is each morning when I wake up healthy with my husband and babies by my side.

The true celebration is watching my clients SOAR and discover their soul purpose and genuinely start to nurture and respect themselves and their gifts, regain the confidence to share themselves with the world.

The true celebration is lunch with my brother as we discuss our next business idea.

The true celebration is the feeling of service and impact in the depths of my heart and soul as I fall asleep each night and wake up each morning.

The true celebration is YOU, reading or listening to this book and KNOWING that ABSOLUTE ABUNDANCE is possible and available FOR YOU.

OTHER THINGS I DO AND YOU CAN TOO, TO MEET YOUR ABUNDANCE

Practise Receiving

Our divine feminine right of receiving. Start noticing in your life where you are repelling things. Maybe it's something as simple as a compliment. What do you say when some offers you a genuine heartfelt compliment?

Do you respond with a gracious and wholesome thank you? Were you and receive their kind words like a gift or do you promptly respond with, *"Oh but I feel like crap, my hair is everywhere, and I barely slept last night, look at these bags under my eyes!"*

Obviously, I exaggerated that, but most people can rarely simply receive a genuine compliment graciously so how do you expect to receive more of the bigger things in life?

As always, with working with me, we start with bite size chunks of things you do daily, and I train your brain to respond differently. That way when we get to the big things (like a $80k month), it's just the next organic and natural step in the process.

Unfortunately, most of you won't even start because you make it too hard from the get go. You focus on things outside of yourself or outside of your control and end up frustrated, exhausted and back being stuck.

Let's keep it simple.

Your homework is to receive compliments this week graciously.

Maybe it's hard for you to receive income for your personal products or services?

I realised recently, that's why I did network marketing for so long, I was hiding behind someone else's brand and product. Once I stepped out and created my own personal brand, this is when my business scaled and grew.

Obviously, I didn't consciously know I was "hiding."

One day on my morning walk in my morning routine, I had another ah-ha moment. A real life changing moment! Are you hiding behind something so you don't have to put a price on yourself? Hmmmm, food for thought.

Create A Personal Brand
Stop hiding behind fashions, fads, network marketing, relationships, an identity (being a mum) a job or whatever else it is you are hiding behind. Start a personal brand that is aligned with the essence of YOU. Create a following with your authentic brand and you serve the community with your conscious products and services and people will be magnetised to your work and buy from you.

Pay Off Your Debts
Pay off or create realistic payment plans for your debts. To start receiving income in your business or for your products and services. Start paying for the ones you are currently using with love and gratitude. This is ripple into your clients and most of them will start to pay you with love and gratitude.

Pay Yourself First
Always put 10% into an Automated Savings Fund. 10% of everything you earn, straight into an account that you never withdraw from. Most people's financial blueprint is to get

paid and the bank account spikes and then they pay bills and it drops. It's a gradual, SLOW incline (or for some of you a decline if you spend more than you create!).

The automated savings is for when the shit-hits-the-fan moments in life. And trust me it will, so it's comforting to have several months of your expenses covered. When my mentor told me to do this, I was like, *"Yeah right dude, my husband is an International Airline Pilot, he is never gonna lose his job!"*

Luckily, I did it anyway so when the shit did hit the fan for our family, we had a few months expenses covered which took the desperation and pressure off for us to start making life changing decisions together. So, GET OFF YOUR BUTT and set up your automated savings account. NOW.

You will not notice 10% of your wage or income missing. You will adapt your lifestyle to suit accordingly and once again, this will help in growing your wealth portfolio. It also raises your internal financial thermostat as you look at it every now and again you see a sharp, consistent, incline with your finances. It changes something in your subconscious.

Change Your Relationship With Money
Most of us aren't very nice to money. We say things like, money makes you greedy, evil people have money, there is never enough, it causes fights…

I imagine money as a person and if I said all those things to it, it wouldn't want to come and hang out with me. I would repel it and it would avoid me! So, I changed my money story by writing a letter to money and asking it to forgive me for all the mean things I had said and done to it. I then went on to heal my relationship by writing all the amazing fun things we could do together and invite it back into my life to share, contribute and grow together.

Clean Out Your Handbag
Your handbag or wallet is a home for your money. What is the current state of your handbag or wallet? Is it full busting at the seams with no space for anything else to fit in? Bulging with old receipts and discount vouchers, heavy with a load of old cards you don't use anymore? Your wallet is the home for your money, so take a moment to clear it out, get rid of anything you don't use, make it clear, clean and inviting for more money to come play and stay! Money likes organisation and structure so start with your handbag and wallet.

Fill Your Wallet With Money
Do you keep money in your wallet or is it empty? My mentor once told me to keep the amount I want to earn a day in cash in my wallet. My first thought was sheer horror.

What if I lost it? What if someone stole it? One million dollars a year is $2800 a day so I apprehensively put that amount in my wallet. Once I worked through the fear, I realised having money in my wallet reminded me every time I opened my wallet of its presence. It started to feel normal! I challenge you to try it! Fill your wallet with the amount of money you would like to create per day.

Spend less than you make.

Schedule time to manage your money, every single day.

I used to have a miserable relationship with money. There was never enough, and it was a constant battle to make ends meet. Even when I first started my business, I felt like I spent most of my time chasing my tail.

I had done a few things on the checklist and avoided the others as they seemed to hard, or I didn't know how or legitimately didn't have the time to do them. I didn't have time to do them because I didn't prioritise money as it was lowest in my values. I was so blocked, I just didn't know what to do next. So, I asked myself, *"What do I do well?"* and my answer was HEALTH. My health, I prioritise my health so the next thing I asked was, *"What do I do in my health that makes it successful?"*

My answers came straight away:

1. Make time for it. Schedule it.
2. Prioritise it.
3. Spend time on it. Every day.

So, I decided I would model the way I made health work for me to my money. I added to my checklist: "Make time for money." I scheduled 30 minutes every morning in my calendar (just like I did for my workouts, which were at 4am mind you!).

Side Note: I invite you to take a second now to recognise the area of life you do best. Where you are most organised and structured, that you enjoy and is working well for you.

Write you answer here:

_____

Now ask yourself what do I do in _____
that makes it successful?

_____

_____

_____

And now you have your personalised answer on how to make your finances or lower priority areas of your life work more efficiently.

So, the first thing I had to do was:

1. Make time for my finances. Schedule it.

I entered it into my calendar at 9am every day: "Check finances," which was boring, uninspiring and I avoided or made an excuse to skip most days.

As it wasn't having the desired effect I thought, what else could I call it to make it more enticing, interesting and at least a possibility of enjoying it? I changed it in my calendar at 9am everyday to "MONEY MATTERS."

Simply by changing the language, it changed the way I felt about it. Now at the start of every day, I'm excited to start my day with MONEY MATTERS.

I spend a minimum of 30 minutes at the start of every day paying my bills with gratitude, invoicing my clients with love, allocating payments and doing my mindful MONEY MATTERS. I also use this time to clean out my wallet and handbag weekly. I have a bookkeeper and an accountant who I meet with once a month.

Each day, I check in with money because it DOES MATTER. The more I have, the more I can give.

I hear a lot of you say, *"I'm already happy, I don't need money to be happy,"* (which is what I also used to say!)

So, if you're already happy, why not just have it then?

Millionaire Mum

ABUNDANCE Checklist:

DESCRIPTION	DONE
GET CLEAR - VISUALISATION "WHAT DOES A MILLIONAIRE LOOK LIKE?"	☐
PRACTICE RECEIVING - START WITH RECEIVING COMPLIMENTS	☐
STOP HIDING BEHIND NETWORK MARKETING - IDENTITY RELATIONSHIP	☐
CREATE PERSONAL BRAND	☐
PAY OFF DEBTS (OR CREATE REALISTIC PAYMENT PLANS) PAY YOURSELF FIRST SET-UP AUTOMATED SAVINGS ACCOUNT	☐
WRITE A LETTER TO MONEY	☐
CLEAN OUT FOR HANDBAG & WALLET	☐
SPEND LESS THAN YOU MAKE	☐
SCHEDULE TIME EVERYDAY TO DO "MONEY MATTERS"	☐

DIANE MCKENDRICK
AUTHOR - LIFE COACH - SPEAKER

SUMMARY:

- Most people's dominant state is one of burnout and feeling exhausted, overwhelmed. Spreading yourself so thin and wondering how to "make it all work."

- You see something in my life that you desire for yours.

- The full truth encompasses both sides. Perceived Positive and negative. Most people attach to positive and reject negative. Absolute Abundance is accepting both.

- Most people associate Abundance with the metrics, numbers, tangible assets. True abundance is a vibration.

- People speak of abundance mostly in the realm of money. Absolute Abundance is a wholesome approach to ALL areas of life and understanding they all intertwined together.

- Abundance is NOT in the future, it is in the NOW.

- Abundance is a contagious frequency.

- The more that you have, the more you get. The more that you get, the more that you give. The more you give, the more you get!

- When you match on the inside the thing you desire on the outside it will be presented to you.

- Abundance is an inside job.

- $20k, $60k and $150k months are all different vibrations. They feel different.

- Abundance is here for us people. All around us. Waiting for us to meet it but too many of us are stuck in the story, excuses and programming to meet it.

Chapter Ten

COMPELLING NEW IDENTITY: YOU ARE HER AND SHE IS YOU

"You have to be still to hear her and most people are too busy being busy to hear her."
Diane McKendrick

You have made it all the way to the last chapter... CONGRATULATIONS!

I trust you have taken the time to do the exercises, open your heart and commit to the Greatness that is inside of you.

You have laughed and cried through the pages of this book with me and now it's time for YOU to choose YOUR path.

To stand up and be SEEN and heard.

To create your Millionaire Mum moment; whatever that is to YOU.

As you read or listen to the pages of this book and complete the exercises, something inside of you is changing; transforming. No matter how long it took you to read or listen to this, one thing is consistent for ALL of us.

The woman you were, when you picked this book up for the first time, is vastly different to the WOMAN you are NOW.

Likewise, the woman I was when I started writing this book is vastly different to the woman I am NOW.

You may not feel much difference, mostly because you aren't aware of the changes and they have been so subtle. I don't feel much different, either. As you take a moment to reflect, however, you will feel the expansion.

Take a moment to feel it NOW.

Remember back to the very first moment when you picked this book up.

Compelling New Identity: You Are Her And She Is YOU

Where were you? What were you thinking? How were you feeling?

Now tune in to how you feel right NOW. Likely you are buzzing from within ready to take the leap. Trusting yourself and the process as you navigate the next part of your journey. Exhilarated and deeply devoted to yourself and the difference you can make in this world.

Simply by being and doing YOU!

Take a moment to acknowledge all the growth and learnings from the stories, concepts and strategies I have shared in this book. Some you may have been familiar with, others have been completely new to you.

How does it feel to you now? The idea of a random normal day-to-day mum or woman (just like YOU) writing a book about being a Millionaire, when she's not... Yet.

Imagine how terrified I was of starting, launching, sharing and publishing this book. The little voice in my head reminding me of the negatives - the whole time...

What if you can't? What if you fail? What if it's a flop?

You're not even a millionaire! What a fraud! You should be ashamed of yourself!

This voice has been loud and persistent, and through the writing of this book, I have discovered a different relationship with it. It was so persistent it nearly broke me down, I nearly gave up several times, the stress was taking such a toll on me.

It was on one of my early morning walks when it was going bananas on me.

It was as I started to write the third chapter. The voice patronising and berating me consistently. I was struggling to show up to write every day because I simply was crippled in fear, utterly debilitated.

I felt like a fraud and that everyone would laugh in my face.

As the voice continued to tell me everything (in detail) that was wrong with me and remind me of absolutely every tragic, traumatic possibility that may unfold, I stopped walking.

I turned to the direction I heard the voice from and I finally answered it.

I stopped moving the voice to the back seat of the car to silence it and turned to it and said out loud, *"Well, what if? What if all that terrible stuff happens? What are WE going to do about it?"*

THE VOICE STOPPED. THE CLOUDS PARTED – LITERALLY!

And there was silence for the first time in my life.

It was a timeless and spaceless moment where I lost track of time and have no idea how long I was standing there for. The next thing I heard was, *"Thank you. Thank you for listening to*

Compelling New Identity: You Are Her And She Is YOU

me. I've been trying to get your attention for years. Of course, WE will know what to do. Carry on, WE got this!"

So, I gathered up ALL the voices in my head and I carried on. Although it was only brief and that voice still pipes up every now and again, I have a different relationship to it now.

Obviously, this is a metaphor for my ego. The part of our brain that keeps us safe. She is just doing her job and pointing out the danger on the way, so I can be aware of it.

Most of us will STOP there. We will get lost and distracted in the scarcity and fear. It will stop us taking action, keep us procrastinating and making excuses.

You have a choice to make.

You can become entangled and intimate with those voices and listen to them, react to them, or just be aware of them, thank them and move on. Understand that they are there to keep you safe and they're playing an important role by warning you. Get off the roundabout.

I want to know which part of myself stopped me in the street that day to acknowledge the ego?

To break the pattern of being in my head and separating that part of myself from myself. My knowing and "Compelling New Identity." The wise woman within who knows. That's who.

Often as I mentioned early in the book, she is talking to you, too. In a whisper, so you don't often hear it. But she is there. You have to be still to hear her and most people are too busy being busy to hear her. Distracting ourselves with social media, work, drama, conflict, food, alcohol or whatever vice you use to dull it.

What do you do to stop yourself from connecting with your higher self?

The thing stopping you from your own Millionaire Mum moment (or whatever is important to you) is the distance between where you are and where you desire to be.

In fact, I am having a Compelling New Identity Crisis right now. I am so close to finishing this book and sending it off to the first edit. I literally have half a chapter to go!

So close yet so far. There is something holding me back. Something is blocking me.

I find myself procrastinating, making excuses, sitting at the computer for hours and typing and then deleting what I typed or staring blankly at the screen thinking, *"Ahhh, what can I write?"*

Nothing seems good enough.

Nothing is deep or powerful enough to put my feelings into words.

It's been months.

I've done all the strategies, EFT Tapping, timeline therapy, leveraged the pain of not getting it done, visualisation, meditation, fear neutralisation... I even just walked out to Gus and asked him, *"Can you please coach me through this?"*

I know that part of my blockage is that I am still thinking, feeling, planning, writing and sharing from my OLD IDENTITY. This is why it doesn't feel right; she doesn't know how or what to write in this chapter.

In order to finish this book, I have to dive even deeper into my Millionaire Mum identity. I need to embody her, trust her, meet her, nourish her and BE HER.

I am going to use this blockage and my own process in finishing this book to portray and share my teachings on this topic.

Upon reflection, this is one of most relevant and powerful processes I take my clients through. Similar to me being blocked on creating this final chapter for you, many of my clients come to me with paralysing fear and procrastination patterns. Sometimes to the point where they create self-sabotage injuries, illness, and drama, all to avoid "writing the last chapter."

For some of them, it is starting a fitness and nutrition routine, for others it's buying their dream home or land package. Recently, it's been with a fellow Millionaire Mum stepping into the big league and taking her 6-figure bookkeeping business to 7-figures by hiring a team, getting her time back, doubling her income and halving her time at work; a single Mum, with 2 kids, doing what she loves and taking the massive leap in her life and business.

Just last week, I helped another Mumma who I have been working with for less than a year leave her full-time job of 16 years and move into her "hobby" personal training business full time. Her business is now replacing her full-time job income and she has more time and energy to spend with her husband and children, whilst sharing her knowledge, essence and energy with the world. Building her own community supporting women in their health and fitness journey her Purpose in life.

One of my all-time favourites is the gorgeous lady who came to me for what she thought was to grow and scale her business and within three weeks of working with me, she called her beloved partner into her life.

Or beautiful JMP, Evolution Coach who wrote the testimonial for this book, quadrupling her wholesome, heartfelt business in less than three months, all while working full time and designing her life around time with her gorgeous, young family.

There are so many more sacred celebrations I can share with you!

You will literally have your experience RIGHT NOW.

There is something you are pressing pause on before you start because there is a part of you that just doesn't know. Similar to me finalising this chapter.

It's time to fully and intimately meet my COMPELLING NEW IDENTITY. As it is, yours.

Compelling New Identity: You Are Her And She Is YOU

Until you understand this, you are accessing your information, actions and how you interpret your next step from the OLD and in order to rise to the next level and vibration, we have to lean in and meet THE NEW WOMAN.

The wise one, the one that knows.

She is waiting for you to connect with her.

The answers are within you right now, we just have to change the way we access them because it's different now.

YOU ARE READY.

I AM READY.

WE ARE READY.

She is there waiting to be met. Let's take the time to meet her right now!

The old me was putting so much pressure on myself on how to share all the content, processes, checklist and audios which I personally created, as I deepened my intimate bond with my Compelling New Identity and my future self.

Part of my procrastination was that, I wanted to share it ALL in this book detailing exactly what I did to overcome my fear, meet myself, draw the line in the sand and step over it.

It isn't the right format for a book and logistically too hard to compress to the pages of a book. Spreadsheets, checklists, videos, meditations… Trust me, I tried to get it all in here for you, but it is going to be so much more value to you set out easily on the computer.

I have created a Step by Step Guide of ALL the processes I personally went through in REAL TIME as I was writing this chapter. I have them all organised and set out on the Mastermind dashboard for you to make your way through in your own time. Every single thing I did to MEET HER and finish this chapter and book.

One of the strategies I created which is easy enough to share from the book is my "Get To Know Her Questionnaire," which I will share below.

Before I do here is a reminder:

You are closer than you have ever been to meeting and being the GREATEST YOU.

Often, we identify with ourselves from our past and at a deep subconscious level we live from the programming, perceptions and events that have "shaped us" in the past.

You may not realise this is your deep belief, however you know the pain, trauma and drama which is ever present around you. No matter what you do, how many books you read, how much meditation or chanting you do, you just can't seem to crack the code.

This pattern may be playing out in one or several areas of your life.

Compelling New Identity: You Are Her And She Is YOU

As humans, what we're naturally designed to do is to scan the past to predict the future...

Like a computer, the input determines the output. Which leaves a lot of us accessing, perceiving and receiving information of pain, trauma and which is communicated to us from our younger, immature, wounded self. Often this perpetuates tragedy, loss, drama and trauma.

We are wired to keep repeating the SAME THING. Even if it's painful, shocking, or traumatic!

On the other end of the spectrum, some of you may want to take massive leaps in your life, business, health or finances and there is something blocking you. You can't quite "put your finger on it" - but it's there.

Similar to my experience with writing this last chapter; so close yet so far.

To change the outcome, I needed to change the input. In order to change the input coming in, I changed the part of myself I was asking for the guidance. And I'm inviting you to do the same thing.

Initially, I was connecting to my current or past self. Recently, I realised that it was my future self I needed to check in with direction and guidance in my next leap in life and the last chapter of my book.

This Mastermind Module and chapter is dedicated to helping myself AND you create an Intimate Bond with your "Future

Self," getting you to create and connect deeply within to your KNOWING and REMEMBERING and letting that be your light house; your soul compass now.

Take a moment now to tune into her.

Start with this questionnaire I created half way through this chapter to support me in creating the intimate bond with my Future Self, so she could guide me in finishing this book.

Compelling New Identity: You Are Her And She Is YOU

QUESTIONNAIRE

Answer these questions for your DREAM LIFE as if it is all exactly as you dreamed what would it look, feel, and sound like.

Uncage yourself and let your imagination run WILD; you're answering this from an ANYTHING IS POSSIBLE place.

How does she feel?

Who is in her physical space?

Who is in her physical space?

What can she hear?

What can she see?

What is her first thought in the morning?

What is the first thing she does when she gets out of bed?

What time does she wake up?

How does she wake up?

If you have found this helpful, I would like to offer you FREE 7-day access to the Mastermind so you can complete the module and meet YOURSELF.

SUMMARY:

- You have made it to the end and now it's time for YOU to choose your path. To stand up and be SEEN and heard. To create your Millionaire Mum moment (whatever that is to YOU).

- The woman you were, when you picked this book up for the 1st time, is vastly different to the WOMAN you are NOW.

- It's time to stop resisting the voices in your head and acknowledge them instead.

- One of those voices, usually the quietest is your FUTURE SELF trying to connect with you.

- Most people are "too busy" or numb distracting themselves with social media, work, drama, conflict, food, alcohol to hear her.

- I was blocked finishing this chapter because I wasn't listening to her yet. I was stuck in fear.

- Some people with paralysing fear will create procrastination patterns even to the point where they create self-sabotage injuries, illness, drama all to avoid "writing the last chapter."

- There is something you are pressing pause on RIGHT NOW before you start because there is a part of you that just doesn't know. Similar to me finalising this chapter and my clients. It's time to fully and intimately meet my COMPELLING NEW IDENTITY.

- We are designed to access information, actions and therefore decisions from the PAST. In order to rise to the next level and vibration we have to lean in and meet THE NEW WOMAN.

- YOU ARE READY

- I AM READY

- WE ARE READY

- You are closer than you have ever been to meeting and being the GREATEST YOU.

So, here it is my friends! Together, we've collectively reached the end of this book!

I wrote about being a Millionaire, long before I was one! Maybe some of you are reading this a few years down the track or perhaps you where one of the many who followed the journey from the start and got your book on Presale! Regardless of when you joined the journey or the community, I want to finish this book by reminding you that:

YOU CAN DO ANYTHING.

You deserve unconditional happiness, freedom, love, abundance and everything your heart desires.

Declare it boldly NOW to the universe, reach out and if you want a higher level of support to be connected to a conscious community, please contact me personally on social media.

I have finished this book and I am one step closer to being a Millionaire Mum.

I have declared boldly to the universe, designed my life and business around my soul purpose and I am leaving a legacy for my children.

I can have my cake and eat it too, and so can you. TAKE THAT FIRST BITE!

Love and light, always,

Diane

ACKNOWLEDGEMENTS

A deep appreciation and expression of love and gratitude to EVERYONE I have crossed paths with over the past 41 years; every conversation, interaction and connection has been the catalyst to create a life, community and legacy of empowering people to peel back the layers and REMEMBER their own power. To choose life and stop reacting to it. To understand that you are governed by an internal set of rules that you didn't consciously choose for yourself and that NOW is the time to wake up from the slumber.

Firstly, to my husband, my best friend, my lover, my confidant and my biggest fan. You believed in me long before I believed in myself. You are the most caring, considerate, warm and gentle man. The wind beneath my wings, Angus McKendrick. You always hold me in the highest vision of myself and are my daily reminder of true love. The first time we locked eyes, I was lost in your gentle, deep blue eyes - I knew I was home. You look into my soul, have my heart hold my hand - every day I am grateful for you.

Thank you for believing in me on the days I didn't believe in myself. Thank you for always reminding me I am enough. Thank you for being sturdy and strong with softness and grace.

You are my favourite, the kiss to my hug, the seed to my pod. Thank you for taking my hand and standing by my side.

To my children, Ross and Esme, my little people. This book is for you. To remind you that you are perfect, whole and complete, just the way you are. To dream big and always stay true to you. To be your own observer and be a friend to the voices in your head.

Always remember, "Mummy loves you," and there is always sunshine on the other side of the clouds. Choose your life. Speak your truth, question everything and do things even when they are hard, even when they are scary.

My world is a better place because you are in it.

To Michelle, Allan and Andrew, my siblings - my reflections, my courage and my JOY. Every day, I thank graciousness that we have this lifetime together, to learn, to grow and to LOVE together.

And lastly, Mum and Dad. THANK YOU FOR loving me.

Acknowledgements

Thank you for teaching me that external things, money, weight, followers are not a metric for success but deep connection to myself and living on purpose, making a difference and caring about people is where the Soul Success sparks.

Thank you for the tough lessons. Thank you for the sacrifices you made and never speak of.

Thank you for teaching me to question everything and that I am the leader of my life.

Thank you for believing in me.

ABOUT THE AUTHOR

Diane McKendrick was born and raised in Ipswich and still resides in Ipswich, Queensland, Australia.

She is the second-eldest of four. Born second to Michelle, her older sister by three years, Diane then graced the world with her presence. Allan was born a few years later and then Andrew joined the family, two years after. The awesome foursome are still best friends, business partners and each other's biggest cheerleaders.

A small-town girl with a big heart, she was a gifted athlete and by the time she was 17, she had represented her state and country in both swimming and running.

Due to an injury, her direction and focus changed; as an 18-year-old, she decided to escape the expectation of going to university and backpacked around the world for two years.

Being of a naturally shy and timid nature, these two years abroad were very exhilarating, frightening and challenging.

Upon returning to Australia, Diane got a job as a receptionist and at a shopping centre, spending the next ten years working her way up to Portfolio Manager of several shopping centres.

She was about to move to Sydney to start her new job when she met a man with blue-as-the-sea eyes on the beach on Australia Day and chose her heart over her head. She decided to remain in Brisbane and married Gus in 2010.

In 2012, Ross was born, then Esme popped out on the lounge room floor, a few years later. (Thanks to Modern Midwifery for the natural, magical home birth experience.)

About The Author

Today, Diane lives in Ipswich with her young family and is close to her extended family. She runs a successful holistic health-based organisation with her family and has an international following. She is a Best-Selling Author, International Motivational Speaker, Podcaster, Life and Business Coach and has her own personal range of clothing, jewellery, and most recently, protein powders.

Diane is a family person who is passionate about bringing the best parts of science, spirituality and soul signatures together to remind humans of their power. To stay true and authentic to yourself and follow your dreams, while filling your cup so you can live the life of your dreams.

Diane spends her days with her family or running national and international Goddess Retreats, Online Masterminds, mentoring programs, writing books, guest speaking, podcasting and is dedicated to helping other amazing women's voices be shared far and wide by supporting them in starting their own heart-centred businesses, and of course; supporting other Mum's, just like you, to achieving and LIVING YOUR BEST LIFE!

DIANE MCKENDRICK
AUTHOR – LIFE COACH – SPEAKER

Diane Mckendrick is an expert in personal empowerment, publishing her first book "RISE UP" in 2018 which became an Amazon Best Seller. She has also published her 2nd book Millionaire Mum in June 2021.

She has become a game changer in the industry, guiding and facilitating people to connect into their true power and unlock their greatness. To monetise the Soul Purpose and create the life of their dreams

Diane is an international guest speaker and author and comes highly recommended with her contagious presence that will wow your audience and leave everyone in the room feeling loved, powerful and ready to change their world.

Online programs, spiritual retreats and one-on-one coaching supported by the message of her Amazon Best Seller books has been the catalyst for supporting many people to click off auto pilot and start creating a fulfilling and financially rewarding life.

Using a combination of science and spirituality, she will help open the flood gates and encourage people to stop merely responding to life and alternatively, using the tools, techniques and strategies she shares, to step into their power, claim their freedom and start creating the life they desire and deserve with absolute certainty.

She has a unique gift of engaging any audience and guiding them into a powerful present and resourceful state.

If you want a personable, dynamic and insightful speaker who connects with your audience, has an uncanny ability to gently but fiercely challenge peoples' model of the world and reframe it into possibility, passion and presence - contact Diane now!

Depending on your needs, she can adapt each presentation to your industry or profession.

For more information, visit:

www.dianemckendrick.com

TESTIMONIALS

"This book bought me to tears. So real and vulnerable and resonated with me so strongly that I got emotional. Diane has a way with words that will change the way you look at yourself and your life."
Michelle Anne, Soul Healer and Fellow Millionaire Mum
www.those2sisters.com

"I've recently started working with Di after one of the hardest years of my life. In three, short months, this woman has saved my life! I was questioning my existence, my purpose and struggling to wake up every day. I have a small business and I lost all faith in not just my business, but life in general. A downwards spiral into despair as even though I have an amazing partner, it became me and my bed outside of work hours. I was at the point where I didn't want to go anywhere or talk to anyone. I even avoided social media because I didn't want to see people living life while I didn't want to live mine. My Mum got me onto Di's podcast and arranged a meeting for me to talk about my concerns and fears.

Di immediately made me feel safe and comfortable. Instantly, I felt supported and not on my own anymore. Within minutes, she magically reminded me of what I truly wanted and desired, that it was ok to want more for myself, my future, my partner, my family and my business. Di has encouraged and supported some of my toughest times in business and my personal life. She really does have a sixth sense in guiding and reminding us of our greatness. She knows how to turn every pain into a lesson, even the smallest ones. In the short time I have worked with Di, I have changed many deep seeded emotional patterns and behaviours. Words can't express how grateful I am for Di and the outlook I now have in life and business.

I have come such a long way and I know I am going to step further into my spiritual awakening and as a result, booming and growing my heart centred and wholesome business, Briella Beautiful. I know that I now have the unshakable support from Those 2 Sisters, Diane and Michelle Anne, and

Testimonials

our conscious community which they have created. Every step of the way I have a hand to hold, shoulder to cry on, or sister to celebrate with, as well as friendships I will treasure forever."
Natasha Shauntelle, Briella Beautiful
www.briella.com.au

"As I contemplated how on Earth I would put into words of the impact Diane has had on my life, I took a deep breath and just listened. My conscious mind said, just command your subconscious to do it at this moment. I received an image from the future. It was in 4D. We were sitting at sunset on the balcony of my million-dollar beach estate home in Port Douglas, with this book on my lap. We were drinking cacao, just in pure gratitude for this moment. I said to Di, remember, back in 2020 when I won that free laser coaching call with you on a spinning wheel and you were writing the book Millionaire Mum? Di said, oh my gosh, yes, I do.

From that moment, I felt compelled to work with you. You got started and quadrupled my business in four months and I said, yes, I do. It's amazing. I said yes, it truly is. And now you and my clients and yours have all created a million-dollar heart-centered business. You truly have left a beautiful legacy.

As the image fades out and I sit here, I know it to be true whilst the book is not yet printed and I have not settled yet on the land. I Know It All To Be True. Diane has taught me how to access my inner power. Connect with my sole purpose, and on a deeper level, neutralize and dissolve my fears.

She has helped me pinpoint and dissolve beliefs that hold me back and techniques to scale up my business while staying in divine flow. She's held me in the power of her community, stared into my soul and showed me my power. The same power that is inside you, as you read this book,

Testimonials

I invite you to open your heart and mind to the possibility of a life where you can be, do and have anything if you just tuned into the wisdom in these pages. Take care. God bless."
Jody Michelle Perry,
Evolution Coach and Fellow Millionaire Mum
https://linktr.ee/JodyMichellePerry

"Diane is an unassuming powerhouse! Hiding behind a seemingly shy exterior, Di possesses an incredibly unique and beautiful skillset that transforms people from stuck to seen! Di gave me the tools to change my life and if you believe in yourself and trust in Di, you can change your life, too!"
Bec Condon (Bec Sta), Fellow Millionaire Mum
Founder of Intents Healing
intentshealing.com.au

JOURNEY WITH ME AND JOIN MY CONSCIOUS COMMUNITY

2 - 4 Day Spiritual Goddess Retreats

Raise your vibrations, increase your vitality and release the Goddess within.

- Women's circle work
- Breakdown to Breakthrough
- Vision Boards with a twist
- Meditation
- Camp Fire
- Full plant-based menu
- Yoga every morning
- Intuitive healings
- Cacao ceremony
- Sound and Voice Healing

If this sounds like your JAM, visit www.dianemckendrick. com to check dates and book your spot now.

Half-Day Workshops - 6 Steps To Soul Success

Join Those2Sisters Michelle Anne and Diane at their next Half-Day Workshop. They will teach you the exact strategies to:

- ↣ Stop feeling LOST and get clarity on your Soul Purpose and WHY you are here
- ↣ Wake up every morning with focus and discipline
- ↣ Stop Procrastinating and get comfortable being uncomfortable
- ↣ Dissolve fear so you can start living your PURPOSE
- ↣ Create more income by doing what you love with people you love

Workout Gear and Protein Powders:

Make your workouts FUN. Grab yourself some of Diane's specially designed workout gear.

Grab a bag of her customised protein blend, which will support busy Mum's in staying fit and healthy.

Podcast - Rise and Shine Podcast:

A podcast where we discuss how to fill your own cup, embrace financial abundance and live the life of your dreams.

Mastermind:

A FREE 7-day link with QR code to access it:

Channelled & intuitively designed by Diane's sister Michelle Anne, these creations are globally anchoring women to their truth & presence. This jewellery was created to assist its wearer to remember her true self & let her emerge. When placing on your finger or around your neck set an intention and with each glimpse throughout the day you will be reminded of your power.

Your healing is the healing of the collective, rise up sister and welcome to the tribe.

WWW.DIANEMCKENDRICK.COM

Diane McKendrick
Author · Speaker · Life Coach

NOTES

Millionaire Mum

Notes

www.ingramcontent.com/pod-product-compliance
Lightning Source LLC
Chambersburg PA
CBHW021433080526
44588CB00009B/514